Praise for *Honoring God in Red or Blue*

In a day increasingly filled with soundbite rants and angry voices, Amy Black offers an alternative—one based on Christian civility. *Honoring God in Red or Blue* will help Christians learn how to maintain their convictions with grace, and press their arguments with love and respect.

—Greg Wheatley, radio host of
Inside Look with Greg Wheatley

Amy Black's combination of practical political experience, scholarly insight, and Christian wisdom is all too rare. If only she were running for president!

—John Wilson, editor, *Books & Culture*

A concise, easy-to-read introduction to how politics works and how Christians should engage it. Amy Black is a sophisticated, gifted political scientist who knows how to make complicated topics clear and understandable. *Honoring God in Red or Blue* is a helpful contribution to the growing body of thoughtful evangelical reflection on political engagement.

—Ronald J. Sider, president, Evangelicals for Social Action
Professor of Theology, Holistic Ministry & Public Policy
at Palmer Seminary at Eastern University

Humility, balance, insight, patience, discernment, civility, faithfulness —these are qualities too often lacking in contemporary American politics. Sadly, they are also often missing as Christian believers talk about politics and engage in political action. Amy Black's well-informed book points to a better way. The strength of its good sense is matched by the broad accessibility of its prose and the

D0027313

thought-provoking quality of its Christian wisdom. It should be a great help in this, and succeeding, election seasons.

—Mark Noll, author; coeditor, *Religion and American Politics: From the Colonial Period to the Present*

For Christian citizens who are weary from the fighting that too often characterizes current engagement in politics and looking instead for a God-honoring approach, Black's book is a healing balm. The good news: God cares about government, and gives it, as well as citizens and other institutions in society important roles to play and corresponding responsibilities to fulfill. This book invites readers not only to hope again, but to think deeply before deliberately taking action.

—Stephanie Summers, CEO, Center for Public Justice

★ ★ ★

Honoring God in Red or Blue:
Approaching Politics with Humility, Grace, and Reason

★ ★ ★

AMY E. BLACK

MOODY PUBLISHERS

CHICAGO

© 2012 by
AMY E. BLACK

All Scripture quotations, unless otherwise indicated, are taken from the *Holy Bible, New International Version®*, NIV®. Copyright ©1973, 1978, 1984, 2011 by Biblica, Inc.™ Used by permission of Zondervan. All rights reserved worldwide. *www.zondervan.com*

All websites listed herein are accurate at the time of publication, but may change in the future or cease to exist. The listing of website references and resources does not imply publisher endorsement of the site's entire contents. Groups, corporations, and organizations are listed for informational purposes, and listing does not imply publisher endorsement of their activities.

Edited by Elizabeth Cody Newenhuyse
Interior design: Ragont Design
Cover design: Smartt Guys design
Front cover photo: Jose Luis Stephens / iStock
Back cover illustration: Cheryl Graham / iStock
Author photo: Kristin Page

Library of Congress Cataloging-in-Publication Data

Black, Amy E.
    Honoring God in red or blue : approaching politics with humility, grace, and reason / Amy E. Black.
        p. cm.
    Includes bibliographical references.
    ISBN 978-0-8024-0487-9
    1. Christianity and politics—United States. I. Title.
BR516.B5157 2012
261.70973—dc23
                                    2012007030

We hope you enjoy this book from Moody Publishers. Our goal is to provide high-quality, thought-provoking books and products that connect truth to your real needs and challenges. For more information on other books and products written and produced from a biblical perspective, go to www.moodypublishers.com or write to:

Moody Publishers
820 N. La Salle Boulevard
Chicago, IL 60610

1 3 5 7 9 10 8 6 4 2

Printed in the United States of America

To Anna
May you grow in humility and
grace as you seek to honor God.

Contents

★ ★ ★

Introduction

Politics isn't about big money or power games; it's about the improvement of people's lives.

—PAUL WELLSTONE

Government is the problem, not the solution!" "Who knows better how to spend your money, the fat cats in Washington or you?" "The government that does the least protects the most." How often have you heard comments and slogans like these?

When elected officials try to scale back government programs, however, critiques resound from a different side. "They're slashing budgets with a machete, not a scalpel!" "Why should government help the rich on the backs of the poor?" Some problems are so vast and entrenched, these activists contend, that only government can find a solution.

Such stark political differences often blur in the wake of a catastrophe. Natural and man-made disasters can be a unifying force as critics from the political right and left demand a swift and full-force response from government. After Hurricane Katrina and the resulting flooding that affected about 1.5 million people, displaced more than 800,000, and caused an estimated 125 billion dollars in damage, critics protested that federal, state, and local governments did not do enough to help. When the explosion on the Deepwater Horizon offshore drilling platform sent more than 5 million barrels of oil gushing into the Gulf of Mexico, public outcry once again demanded that the president and the government do more to manage the crisis.

Debates rage over the proper size and scope of government. We disagree about which issues and entities need to be under some sort of government control, and which should be left to individuals, businesses, and families to manage for themselves. We know that government is necessary to meet basic needs, protect the people, and provide a safe and stable community. But we disagree about how far government should reach before it violates fundamental rights and freedoms. We want enough government to provide safety and stability, but we also want to be free to make our own choices. This book begins from the premise that a well-functioning government is indispensable, explaining and defending the need for a government strong enough to provide for its people but weak enough to allow citizens and institutions to thrive. In the chapters that follow, you will learn that God cares about politics and government, that our political system offers one important means for loving our neighbor, and that we as Christians can honor God in how we approach politics.

Staking My Claim

Many books discuss religion and politics, but almost all of them have a political agenda, baptizing a particular political party as speaking for God. Most of the voices in the public square distort the truth, demonize opponents, and discourage open and honest discussion. My goals are quite different. First, I want you to be a faithful witness for the gospel as you interact in politics. Second, I want you to develop your own thoughtful and faith-informed perspective on political issues.

Many of us want to move beyond the rants and attacks so commonplace in politics today. This book will help you do this, pointing you to better ways to talk about politics. In our journey together, we'll identify key points of tension that make political dialogue so difficult and consider practical, straightforward ways we can engage in political discussions, analyze political issues, and evaluate candidates as powerful witnesses for Christ.

★ ★ ★

This book begins from the premise that a well-functioning government is indispensable, explaining and defending the need for a government strong enough to provide for its people but weak enough to allow citizens and institutions to thrive.

★ ★ ★

Instead of telling you what you ought to think, this book will give you tools and practical advice to help you apply your faith to politics. I have no hidden agenda to convince you to vote for Republicans or for Democrats. My goal is for you to search the Scriptures and seek guidance from the Holy Spirit to show you how God wants you to honor Him in politics with humility, grace, and reason.

Christians can and will disagree about the proper size and scope of government, which political issues are most important, and the best way to achieve important goals. We should express our convictions with clarity as we engage in vigorous political debates and seek opportunities to influence the political process. But as we think and talk about politics, we must never lose sight of our ultimate goal: honoring God.

PART 1

★ ★ ★

In Defense of Politics

Chapter 1

* * *

Let's Talk! Bringing the Taboo to the Table

If you would win a man to your cause, first convince him that you are his sincere friend.

—ABRAHAM LINCOLN

O ne need not be well-versed in the intricate details of proper etiquette to know some basic truths about the unspoken rules of "polite" conversation. There are two topics that a polite guest never mentions at a dinner party: politics and religion.

Why might etiquette books warn people to steer clear of these subjects? People often have deeply held beliefs about religion and politics, so discussions of such intensely personal topics can quickly become divisive and uncomfortable. Instead of initiating a conversation that could lead to frustration and anger, it may seem wiser to avoid such subjects altogether. But silence or shouting matches are not the only options. If we can find ways to think and talk about religion and politics that won't automatically cause friction, perhaps we can be less afraid to bring these topics to the table.

Although Miss Manners may warn against discussing either of these subjects, the purpose of this book is to defy those rules of etiquette and encourage you to talk about them. This book will help you find appropriate ways to break from the social convention and talk more, not less, about religion and politics.

As a professor of American politics teaching at a Christian college, I think about the connections between religious and political perspectives every day. Although this task is not always comfortable or easy, it is not only valuable—it is essential. Religious values and beliefs directly and indirectly affect how most Americans think about politics. To contribute productively to contemporary debates about American politics, we need to understand both the role of religion and the purpose and limitations of government.

This book is designed to help you navigate the rocky waters of religion and politics so you can engage in lively and fruitful conversations. The chapters that follow will help you address questions such as: How should my Christian perspective affect my political views? How should I respond when I see Christian leaders disagree about politics? Should Christians just avoid politics altogether? How should my faith affect my voting decisions and political participation? On this journey, you will learn more about the American political system and how your faith can inform your political views and actions.

Religion and Politics, "American Style"

Anytime we begin to talk about a serious topic, it is useful to know where everyone is coming from. We cannot help but bring our own perspectives, life stories, and viewpoints into a discussion. We all have ideas about how the world works and what we think is most important, and these ideas help shape our understanding of those around us. If three people are discussing effective parenting techniques, it is useful to know that one has three teenagers, another has a toddler and a baby, and the third has no children. Each person can contribute important insights to the conversation, but their views will likely, in part, reflect their personal experiences.

Let me begin our conversation together by mentioning three

of my starting points. I will introduce some of my underlying assumptions about the role of religion in the United States to help you better understand the perspective that will guide the rest of my discussion.

The United States Is, and Has Always Been, a Nation of Many Faiths

Any frank discussion of religion in contemporary American politics must begin with the recognition that the United States is not, nor ever has been, exclusively Christian. The Constitution created a democratic government designed to protect individual freedoms. Freedom of religion, one of those cherished liberties, is a foundational principle of American democracy.

Given the religious diversity of the United States, we should not expect everyone to accept nor to embrace political arguments that appeal exclusively to Christian principles and doctrine.

★ ★ ★

People from a wide diversity of faiths live in the United States and participate in American politics. According to recent survey data, about three of four adult Americans identify themselves within the Christian tradition, but dozens of other religions also have a place here. Consider one example: The number of Americans identifying as Muslims, Buddhists, and Hindus has more than doubled in the past decade alone. These three religions combined now represent about the same percentage of the population as Jews. The religious group growing most rapidly is seculars, those who say they are not religious at all.

This book approaches the subject of religion and politics in the United States with an awareness of and appreciation for our nation's religious diversity. Just as I want the government to protect my freedom to worship as I choose, so must I promote policies that respect the rights of others to practice their religion. Furthermore, given the religious diversity of the United States, we should not expect everyone to accept nor to embrace political arguments that appeal exclusively to Christian principles and doctrine. Religious views and traditions can and should inform our political perspectives; indeed, the purpose of this book is to help you apply your faith to your politics with care and discernment. But even as we approach politics and government as Christians, we should do so aware that we are engaging in conversations with people from a wide range of perspectives.

Religion Affects Everyone's View of Politics

A second underlying assumption builds from the first. Although some people may think that their religious views have little influence on their thoughts on politics, in practice this is rarely, if ever, the case. Views of religion, notions of right and wrong, and beliefs about the existence of a god or gods and life after death all affect politics, either directly or indirectly.

Consider a few examples of religion directly influencing politics. Some pastors, priests, rabbis, and other religious leaders teach their faithful to support particular political issues and candidates. Many people talk informally about politics when they gather for worship or other congregational events. At some houses of worship, interest groups distribute voter guides that "compare" candidates for office on a few select issues, sending a clear directive about which candidate deserves the vote.

Because religious beliefs provide a basis for morality, religion also has an indirect but significant influence over political views.

In much the same way that religious teaching helps us discern right from wrong in everyday life, it also offers a framework for evaluating a legislative proposal, comparing candidates for office, or assessing the latest actions of the local school board. Even those who do not identify with a particular religion still uphold some form of moral code that, much like an explicitly religious world-view, will affect their approach to politics.

The Ultimate Christian Calling Is to Love God and Follow Him

If religion really affects everyone's views of politics but we don't all share the same religious views, how do we reach enough agreement to govern effectively? Although the context of American politics makes it difficult to reach democratic consensus, I believe that Christians can serve important roles in shaping and guiding both politics and the wider culture. These beliefs lead to my third starting point: politics and government are important, but the most important Christian calling is to love God and follow Him.

As participants in a representative democracy, we need to learn about politics and government to help us make positive civic contributions, but influence in government and politics should never be our primary goal. Political power is enticing and potentially very dangerous; the lure of power can quickly turn us away from serving God. In politics as in all endeavors, Christians must not lose sight of their ultimate purpose.

In his classic writing *On Christian Teaching*, Augustine writes to a young church trying to interpret Scripture correctly and avoid heresy. He points to love as the guiding principle of Christianity, reminding his readers of Jesus' explanation when asked what was the greatest commandment: "'Love the Lord your God with all your heart and with all your soul and with all your mind.' This is the first and greatest commandment. And the second is like it: 'Love your neighbor as yourself.' All the Law and the Prophets hang on these two commandments" (Matthew 22:37–40). Keeping in mind what Augustine calls the "double love" of God and neighbor will help us discern God's truth from false teaching and provide a guide for Christian thought and action.

Honoring God in Politics and Government

Where should we look for guidelines for engaging with politics in ways that demonstrate love for God and our neighbors? What biblical principles can guide us as we seek to honor God in politics and government?

A Blueprint for Politics in the Old Testament

The Ten Commandments provide a helpful starting point. The first commandment calls us to worship God alone, and the second follows from it, prohibiting idolatry:

> *You shall have no other gods before me. You shall not make for yourself an idol in the form of anything in heaven above or on the earth beneath or in the waters below. You shall not bow down to them or worship them; for I, the LORD your God, am a jealous God, punishing the children for the sin of the fathers to the third and fourth generation of those who hate me, but showing love to a thousand generations of those who love me and keep my commandments.* (Exodus 20:3–6)

Only the one true God is worthy of worship, yet other gods capture our attention and fight to take His place. Political power is one such potential idol. If Christians lose confidence in God's sovereign control and instead look primarily to politics to restore society and culture, they can make government into such an idol.

Likewise, the third commandment reminds us of the power and holiness of God and His perfect name: "You shall not misuse the name of the LORD your God, for the LORD will not hold anyone guiltless who misuses his name" (Exodus 20:7). Far more than condemning swearing, this commandment warns against using God's name for anything that does not honor Him.

When defending our political views and actions, we should follow the principles of the third commandment, using God's name with utmost care and reverence. As one pastor explained, "God's answer to a world that blasphemes His name is a community who honors His name. Honoring the Lord's name is our highest calling. Christ will be honored when the world sees a community of people who show awe and affection for Him."[1] In politics as in all spheres of life, we should honor God and serve as light to the world.

A Blueprint for Politics in the New Testament

In much the same way that the first three commandments offer principles to guide Christians who are thinking about politics and government, New Testament passages also provide important insights. Many commentators rightly direct believers to Paul's discussion of civil authority in Romans 13. Although this passage provides a useful description of God's provision for government, when I am asked what biblical text I find most practical for developing a Christian approach to politics, I point first to a different passage, 1 Corinthians 12 and 13.

In this letter, Paul encourages and instructs the church in Corinth, a church struggling with internal division and with a culture fixated on status and power. As one commentator observes, "Paul's purpose is not to correct their theology but to get them to think theologically so they would respond properly to their polytheistic, pluralistic culture."[2] We, too, can find guidance in this epistle to help us think theologically about interactions with politics and government.

First Corinthians chapters 11 through 14 offer Paul's teaching on worship, life in community, and spiritual gifts. He is concerned that some in the church are too prideful, and he writes to correct them. In a short detour from the specific topic of spiritual gifts,

Paul reminds the Corinthians that love is the central guiding principle for interaction with God and with one another. Toward the end of this famous description of God's unconditional love, Paul writes:

> *Love never fails. But where there are prophecies, they will cease; where there are tongues, they will be stilled; where there is knowledge, it will pass away. For we know in part and we prophesy in part, but when perfection comes, the imperfect disappears. When I was a child, I talked like a child, I thought like a child, I reasoned like a child. When I became a man, I put childish ways behind me. Now we see but a poor reflection as in a mirror; then we shall see face to face. Now I know in part; then I shall know fully, even as I am fully known.*
>
> *And now these three remain: faith, hope and love. But the greatest of these is love.* (1 Corinthians 13:8–13)

Even as we are reminded of the power and depth of God's love, we are also cautioned of our human limitations. Paul warns against spiritual pride, reminding us that we all "see but a poor reflection as in a mirror" (v. 12). Our own sinfulness and the fallen state of nature cloud our vision. We can look with hope for the day we will "see face to face" and "know fully," for everything will indeed be clear in God's eternal presence. But, in the meantime, life this side of heaven will be marked by confusion and uncertainty.

A Framework for Thinking about Politics

So how might politics look different if viewed through the prism of the first three commandments and 1 Corinthians 12 and 13? Let me suggest four principles to guide a Christian framework for thinking about politics and government.

• *We all "see but a poor reflection as in a mirror" and therefore should exercise genuine humility when discussing politics.*

When politicians speak, they typically speak with great certainty and clarity. We expect our elected officials to act decisively, and their rhetoric reflects these expectations. But certainty can quickly turn to arrogance, especially when combined with religious language. Critics will often say of someone who holds an opposing view: "Who does she think she is? God?"

Biblical examples such as Paul's teaching to the Corinthians suggest a very different model for talking about politics. If indeed we only have partial knowledge, it follows that a Christian perspective on politics should begin in a context of humility and love. As limited humans, we don't have all the answers. Instead of arrogantly proclaiming our political views, we should approach this subject, as all others, with awareness of our limitations and reliance on God's love and wisdom. We can speak from our religious convictions with love and humility, arguing our views with passion but with respect for others.

★ ★ ★

Since we all have imperfect knowledge this side of heaven and we are each created to serve different functions in the body of believers, it follows that Christians may disagree on political issues.

★ ★ ★

THE POWER OF ADMITTING MISTAKES

★ ★ ★

MANY POLITICIANS SPEAK with certainty because they follow an unwritten rule of politics: never admit you're wrong. When problems arise, deflect the blame. West Virginia Senator Joe Manchin broke this rule. Only a month after assuming office, critics dubbed the new senator "No Show Joe" for his absence during Senate votes on two controversial bills. Manchin apologized in a conference call with the media, explaining he had been back home for a long-planned family Christmas celebration. "Let me apologize to anybody and everybody within our listening and reading areas. I'm very sorry for missing the two votes," he said. "[Constituents] were upset; they were upset over what they had heard or the way it was reported. But I take total blame. It was a mistake."[3]

- *The diversity of the body of Christ makes room for Christians to disagree on many political matters.*

God creates each man and woman as a unique bearer of His image, giving each person a distinctive set of talents that glorify God. As Paul reminded the church in Corinth: "But in fact God has arranged the parts in the body, every one of them, just as he wanted them to be. If they were all one part, where would the body be? As it is, there are many parts, but one body" (1 Corinthians 12:18–20). We are created to live and serve in community, so it makes sense that Christians work best when they combine their perspectives and gifts to work together for the common good. Each person has a valuable contribution to offer.

Since we all have imperfect knowledge this side of heaven and we are each created to serve different functions in the body of believers, it follows that Christians may disagree on political issues. One person might have a special concern and care about education, while another is a strong advocate for the environment, and yet another has a passion for tax policy. We can celebrate these passionate perspectives as gifts from God. Let's take the argument even further. Perhaps God even impresses on the hearts of two Christian believers political views that seem, from our limited perspective, direct opposites. Through constructive dialogue and honest listening, Christians with opposing political views can sharpen one another and help inform each other's political perspectives. Think of how discussions of politics within our churches would change if we began conversations with the recognition that our own particular view on a political issue is imperfect and that another person who holds a different view might also have insight from God.

- *The label "Christian" belongs to God and His work, not to validate human efforts like politics.*

Responding to the question of whether Christians in Great Britain should start a Christian political party, C. S. Lewis answered an emphatic no. Invoking the third commandment, Lewis argued that labeling a particular political group "Christian" would misuse God's name:

> The principle which divides [a "Christian" party] from its brethren and unites it to its political allies will not be theological. It will have no authority to speak for Christianity. . . . It will not simply be a part of Christendom, but a part claiming to be

the whole. By the mere act of calling itself the Christian Party it implicitly accuses all Christians who do not join it of apostasy and betrayal. It will be exposed, in an aggravated degree, to that temptation to which the Devil spares none of us at any time—the temptation of claiming for our favourite opinions that kind and degree of certainty and authority which really belongs only to our Faith.[4]

When we attach the Christian label to things that are not from God, we claim for ourselves an authority that rightfully belongs to God alone.

The Christian label is also dangerous in that it uses God's perfect name as a descriptor for something imperfect. In my work on Capitol Hill, I occasionally encountered activists from "Christian" groups behaving in ways that maligned the name of Christ. In one particularly embarrassing episode, representatives of a Christian interest group came to thank a congresswoman for her sponsorship of legislation important to their agenda. At the start of the meeting, the congresswoman inadvertently offended the organization's leader by asking her to introduce herself. The simple question so wounded the leader's pride that she instructed her assistant to call our office and cut off all further cooperation and communication with the congresswoman and her staff. This encounter with public Christians was a harmful witness; indeed, the incident turned the label Christian into an object of ridicule among some staff members.

- *Politics can and should be a means for demonstrating love in action and building the body of Christ.*

Unfortunately, far too many discussions of Christianity and politics end as shouting matches instead of positive and constructive dialogues. An environment that encourages simplifying issues into two positions, "us" versus "them," creates instant enemies, as if anyone expressing an opinion on a political question must be preparing for war. When Christians speak hatefully of another believer, they sin against their Christian brother or sister and harm the unity of the church. When Christians speak with hatred toward someone outside the church or intentionally cause dissension, they damage the reputation of the church and its witness.

Instead of demonizing those who disagree with us, we should approach them in Christian love. In this age of negative campaigning and personal attack politics, it is almost impossible to imagine a political world modeled after the love described in 1 Corinthians 13. How would the tone of politics change if political opponents actually interacted with each other with patience, kindness, trust, and hope? How different would campaign advertisements look if they "did not delight in evil but rejoiced with the truth"? Although Christians are not likely to change the nature of politics overnight, it is indeed possible and praiseworthy to justify political positions in a manner that is not boastful, self-seeking, or rude. If Christians viewed politics as a means for demonstrating love in action as a witness to the world, the way we approach politics could fundamentally change. More importantly, we could live the gospel by demonstrating the transformative power of love in action. Politicians might not be as successful on the campaign trail, but then again, winning office is not the ultimate goal of the Christian life.

Where Do We Go from Here?

Now that I have shared some of my assumptions and suggested some principles to help Christians think about politics, let's briefly look at the journey ahead. The next two chapters bring a few more basics to the table. After explaining how and when compromise might be a good thing, I defend government as an essential part of a strong and vibrant society.

The second part of the book offers a brief overview of the

American political system and how it works. Chapter 4 looks at the different layers and branches of government with which we interact in our daily lives, and chapter 5 explains the role of political parties and ideology. The section ends with a discussion of the role of church and state in theory and in practice.

The third and final section of the book provides tools and resources that will help you connect your faith with politics. Chapter 7 presents different models for relating faith and politics. After offering suggestions for how to handle political disagreements in chapter 8, I then tackle a complicated policy issue: reducing poverty. The section ends with a practical guide for deciding how to vote and a concluding chapter that suggests ways politics can help us accomplish our ultimate goal: demonstrating love for God and neighbor.

Political scientist Harold Lasswell perhaps unintentionally created a new definition of politics with the title of his book: *Politics: Who Gets What, When, and How.* At its heart, politics is all about people and meeting their needs, so politics and government offer Christians a way to live out the commandment to love our neighbors. In the pages that follow, you will learn more about politics and ways that you can honor God with your participation in it. By the time you reach the end of this book, my hope is that you will be better equipped to serve God and serve others. So let's begin.

QUESTIONS FOR DISCUSSION

Reflecting

1. Think of times in the past when you have talked about politics with friends, family, or coworkers. What was one of the most satisfying conversations? What made it so positive? What was one of the most uncomfortable discussions? Why was it difficult?

2. What are some of your central assumptions about the role of religion in the United States? Where did you develop these views? Have any of your assumptions changed over time?

Responding

3. What are some practical ways that politics can help us live out our call to love God and neighbor?

Chapter 2

Getting to Yes:
The Perils and Promises
of Religion and Politics

All government,—indeed, every human benefit and enjoyment, every virtue and every prudent act,—is founded on compromise and barter.

—EDMUND BURKE

When I began work as a legislative aide in Washington, D.C., the U.S. Senate was evenly split between fifty Republicans and fifty Democrats. Republicans controlled my side of the Capitol complex, the House of Representatives, by a razor-thin margin. Tensions between the two political parties were high.

One issue of particular concern to my newly elected boss, Representative Melissa Hart, was abortion. Hart had already established a strong pro-life voting record serving in the Pennsylvania senate, and she wanted to continue promoting this agenda on Capitol Hill.

Although pro-life and pro-choice activists fundamentally disagree on issues such as legal access to abortion, the congresswoman knew from experience that people could work together across political fault lines and find areas of common ground. Concerned about incidents of mothers abandoning their babies,

leaving helpless infants to die if not discovered in time, Hart asked
me to help her write legislation designed to stop this horrific practice and help parents in crisis.

Hart eventually introduced a bill, the Safe Havens Support Act,
which drew support from some of the most conservative and most
liberal members of the House of Representatives. Pro-life and pro-
choice legislators came together in support of a cause with which
they all agreed: saving the lives of newborns. A few interest groups
objected to the bill, including one pro-family organization that
claimed it would encourage mothers to abandon their babies. But
most saw the bill as the congresswoman intended—as a good faith
effort from people on both sides of a controversial issue to work
together on a problem of mutual concern.

★ ★ ★

It is possible to stand firm on Christian
convictions and still make compromises.

★ ★ ★

The congresswoman succeeded in shepherding the key pro-
visions of the Safe Havens Support Act through the legislative
process; they eventually became law. Although her work on this
bill required compromise and willingness to work with legislators who held very different views, the compromise achieved
important goals. Hart didn't find a way to end the practice of
abortion with this particular bill, but she never compromised her
pro-life commitment. By seeking common ground, she found a
way that she and her apparent political opponents could work
together and save lives.

Black, White, and Shades of Gray

Many observers of the political process argue against political compromise, contending that devotion to a cause requires an unwavering stand. But the case of saving abandoned babies is just one example of seeking common ground and holding firm to principles at the same time. It is possible to stand firm on Christian convictions and still make compromises. But it seems to be an anomaly in today's polarizing political world, and often feels unacceptable to Christians. Let's consider why so many Christians think compromise is bad and discover why they are often wrong.

Religion in Black and White

For many of us, our religious identity is an essential part of who we are and how we view the world. Faith helps us distinguish right from wrong, gives meaning to life and death, and guides our daily lives.

Many people naturally think and talk about religion in black and white terms. Religious worldviews often make truth claims, and some truth claims are by definition exclusive. This is certainly the case with Christianity. Jesus teaches with the strongest of moral clarity, telling His followers, "I am the way and the truth and the life. No one comes to the Father except through me" (John 14:6). Not only does He *speak* the truth, Jesus says that He *is* truth. Jesus—and only Jesus—offers salvation and eternal life. Much of Christian belief presents two options: God's way or the wrong way.

Politics in Black and White

Just as religion helps define personal values, so can our identity as politically conservative, moderate, or liberal point to deeply held beliefs about the world and our place in it. Our understanding of the proper role and function of government helps us rank our political priorities and offers guidance for determining what government should (or should not) do to address problems.

Many Americans adopt the political views of those closest to them. From generation to generation, families provide an important context in which we learn about government, political campaigns, and the role of elected officials. For example, one person's earliest memories may include talking about politics at the dinner table, while another person has no recollection of ever discussing politics with anyone during childhood. Friends and coworkers are another source that may help shape our political values and beliefs.

Especially for those from families who held strong political convictions that they eagerly discussed with others, politics may be part of a person's identity. They know what they believe, they hold strong convictions, and they are often surrounded by people who share similar views. It should be no surprise that many people hold black and white views of politics.

The Political Process in Shades of Gray

Although many people perceive their own religious and political views in black and white terms, the everyday practice of politics is shaded with gray. Fundamentally, democracy is about compromise; it is a rather messy process of give and take. People with extreme political differences can find resolution one of two ways: through force of power or through the political process. The hard and important work of politics is seeking common ground, finding a way for people from a range of perspectives to live peaceably with one another.

Consider the day-to-day work of diplomacy. When tensions flare between countries—a military vessel enters contested waters without permission, an international terrorist is discovered hiding on foreign soil, a national legislature passes new laws that raise the cost of imported goods—diplomats get to work. Through back channels and in face-to-face meetings, representatives of the feuding countries make demands, offer concessions, and search for ways to avert a crisis. Ultimately, political leaders have two options to resolve disputes with other countries. They can seek a political solution, or they can use military force. Although most of the deals happen out of the public view, compromise is the currency of international politics and the best way to avert war.

Compromise is also essential in domestic politics. A modern democracy like the United States requires elected officials to work together to find acceptable solutions to complex problems. Legislators try to balance their personal values and perspective with the needs of the people they represent. At the same time, voters, interest groups, businesses, and others demand elected officials meet their particular needs. All of these different voices raising competing concerns create an intense and high-pressure environment.

Even as outsiders are demanding quick fixes, lawmakers must work within a system that is designed to take time. If you think of how long it can take three or four people to decide what to do for fun on a Saturday afternoon, imagine the complexity of getting 218 or more members of the House of Representatives or even just 60 senators to agree on every single word of complex legislation! If and when policymakers can build majority support for a compromise solution, the resulting policy will likely accomplish only some of the original goals and leave everyone slightly unhappy.

Black and White Ideals in a Gray-Shaded World

Religious and political convictions are usually considered in black and white terms—as absolutes. But it is possible, though not always easy, to connect the two in the world of politics.

God's truth is indeed perfect and unchanging, but human applications of it are not. From New Testament times to the present day, groups of believers have been divided in their interpretations of what it means to follow Christ's teachings. The Word of

God is clear, but human attempts to apply biblical principles to everyday living, such as applying faith to politics, are imperfect.

To complicate matters, many politicians and political activists intentionally use extreme language to try and score political points. Legislators, interest group leaders, and other policy professionals are fully aware that the political process requires bargaining and takes time, but they also know from experience what captures public attention and excites voters. They seek attention and rally supporters with demands for instant results and promises not to back down.

Activists and politicians will try to capture our attention in many different ways. It is our responsibility to test their claims, ask difficult questions when needed, and refuse to respond to distortions or lies.

★ ★ ★

Political leaders also know that when they argue their case with moral clarity and impassioned speech, citizens are very likely to respond. Conservative activist Paul Weyrich described this phenomenon from his own experience building support for political causes: ". . . one thing I had learned over the years is that if you sound as if you are morally certain, people will tend to believe you. So whether or not I know what I am talking about, I always try to sound morally certain."[1] Activists and politicians will try to capture our attention in many ways. It is our responsibility to test their claims, ask difficult questions when needed, and refuse to respond to distortions or lies. Christians can and should apply their faith to politics, but we should do so with great care, seeking ways to engage politics with a spirit of grace and truth.

SO LONG, SESAME STREET?

★ ★ ★

THIS WEEK, BUSH proposed a new budget with devastating cuts to public broadcasting. 'Sesame Street' and other ad-free kids' shows are under the knife. So is the independent journalism our country needs." So warned an email message that Moveon.org blasted to its mailing list. In reality, the budget outline proposed cutting government funding for public broadcasting by about 25 percent, a significant cut but hardly a move that would automatically eliminate one of the most popular children's television shows. The email made some over-the-top claims, but it worked, flooding congressional switchboards with calls. This email is an all-too-common example of interest-group rhetoric that complicates the political process and makes it more difficult for elected officials to seek compromise. Blast messages and fundraising appeals often shade the truth, wildly exaggerate the impending gloom and doom, and find every way possible to scare people enough that they respond. A more honest message would not have caused such outrage.

Holding to Truth, Rethinking Compromise?

As we have seen, many people view religion in black and white terms, yet day-to-day political work necessarily involves shades of gray. It often seems impossible to uphold religious truths in a political arena that requires bargaining and compromise. The path is not easy, but we can show love for God and neighbor in the complex and messy world of politics.

It is difficult—but not impossible—for Christian believers to navigate the complexities of politics in ways that honor God. Many people confront the tension between religion and politics and give up. But those who choose to engage their faith in politics can serve as positive witnesses for the gospel. If you are up to the challenge, let me suggest two things to keep in mind that may help you avoid the perils and embrace the promises of religion and politics.

(1) Recognize that religion and politics will often exist
     in tension.

The first step forward is admitting the problem. As Christians, we should expect that our religious beliefs will provide us with broad principles that inform all aspects of our lives, so our faith will likely have an important influence on how we view political problems. But if we bring black and white views simplistically into a complex process shaded in gray, tension is inevitable.

Religious beliefs are a powerful motivator and can bring great energy to political activity. But even if we do what we think is right, we do so as part of a democratic process that makes room for many participants. If we want the right to express our views in the public square, we must also allow for others to have a voice as well. Not everyone will share the same views, so policymakers will make decisions after listening to many perspectives and weighing a range of concerns, including ours.

Furthermore, elected officials often need to negotiate and bargain in order to get things done. If we enter the political arena expecting lawmakers to translate our specific views directly into public policy, we will almost always leave disappointed. If instead we keep in mind that compromise is likely necessary to accomplish political goals, we are more likely to accept the tensions inherent in the process.

(2) We can uphold truth and make political compromises.

The need for political compromise frustrates many Christians seeking change. The Bible teaches truth and provides a moral framework for ordering life, so they worry that they will have to abandon their principles in the political arena. They see compromise as a bad thing.

Not all compromise is problematic. Sometimes it's essential for maintaining healthy relationships, as we all can attest from interacting with family, friends, and coworkers. Siblings learn to share and take turns. Coworkers planning an office event weigh many suggestions before incorporating some of them into a final plan. Marriage partners consider their spouse's interests as well as their own when making decisions large and small. Reaching agreements and solving problems is an essential way we demonstrate love for our neighbor.

Political bargaining also serves laudable goals. It is often (but not always) possible to agree to compromises in the process of crafting new laws without abandoning one's principles and core beliefs.

In one very common form of political bargaining, elected officials sometimes make political concessions because they believe that getting part of what they want is better than achieving nothing at all. Evangelical political observers Stephen Monsma and Mark Rodgers call this type of bargaining a "half-a-loaf compromise" and contend that such deals are often necessary in a fallen and imperfect world. Legislators who choose such tactics need not compromise their fundamental beliefs, nor do they necessarily lose sight of God's truth. As Monsma and Rodgers explain:

God's word is truth. Biblical principles are absolute. But our applications of God's truth are often fumbling and shrouded in the fog produced by extremely complex situations, missing facts, and the pressures of limited time. All this means that when one is asked to compromise by accepting only some of what one is seeking to achieve, one is not being asked to compromise absolute principles of right and wrong.[2]

In many situations, Christians will seek change based on principles grounded in biblical truth. Yet even when we know our principles are right, we still must apply them in the context of an imperfect political system with finite knowledge, seeing "only a poor reflection as in a mirror."

COMPROMISES TO SAVE LIVES: PREVENTING HIV/AIDS

★ ★ ★

AN ESTIMATED 33 MILLION people currently live with HIV/AIDS. In the coming year another 3 million will likely contract the virus, and more than 2 million people will likely die from complications of AIDS. With no known cure and with many of the world's poor unable to access treatment, contracting the virus is usually a death sentence. Almost all experts agree that the only hope for curtailing the loss of life is preventing infections in the first place.

Consensus quickly erodes when discussing prevention programs. Because AIDS is a sexually transmitted disease, the three most common steps toward prevention are promoting abstinence, encouraging sexual fidelity, and distributing condoms to the most vulnerable and those likely to engage in risky behavior. The Christian who believes that abstinence outside of marriage is God's plan will likely support the principles behind the first two steps but may disagree in principle with the third, condom distribution. Yet another biblical principle is also at stake, the belief in the sanctity of human life. Since condoms help save lives by reducing the risk of transmission by 80-90 percent, perhaps compromise makes sense.

For some of those most at risk of infection—young girls and women forced into prostitution, spouses of an infected partner, and victims of abuse—abstinence is likely not an option. Access to potentially life-saving protection offers them some defense from further victimization. In such cases, providing condoms is a small compromise in the name of the larger concern for human life and dignity.

Considering condom distribution for others at risk because of their own lifestyle decisions and choices raises more difficult moral questions. Yet even in this case, the compromise of one set of important values for the goal of saving lives seems worth the price.

Not all political compromise is good; some forms can be quite dangerous. Elected officials often find themselves in situations where they are tempted to set aside their moral and ethical principles in order to achieve personal or political gain. If, for example, a legislator trades votes with a colleague, agreeing to support a bill that goes against her beliefs in order to secure a fellow legislator's assurance of his vote in favor of her bill, she has sacrificed her principles for political gain. Instead of upholding the principle of love for God and neighbor, the legislator is willingly acting against what she believes is right. The political world is full of temptations, and many principled men and women have justified unethical behavior with claims of serving a greater good. But in the end, in politics as in all areas of life, we need to be faithful to our beliefs and hold fast to our principles.

As we have seen, compromise can be a tool for good. Not all compromise is wise or God-affirming, but many forms of day-to-day bargaining are actually opportunities to love our neighbor by seeking common ground and serving others. The compromise and bargaining necessary to maintain a vibrant democracy are hard to achieve, but the benefits are great.

Having considered some of the complexities of mixing religion and politics, we are almost ready to examine how the American system actually works. One more background piece remains: considering the strengths and weaknesses of government.

QUESTIONS FOR DISCUSSION

Reflecting

1. What comes to mind when you hear the word "compromise"? What are some ways that you make compromises as part of your daily life?

2. Do you think and talk about religion in black and white terms? Why or why not? Do you think about the everyday practice of politics as shaded with gray? Why or why not?

Responding

3. Suggest some ways that compromise in politics can be a "tool for good." Think of other ways that compromise might be problematic. How can we determine when it is wise to compromise and when it is unwise?

Chapter 3

★ ★ ★

Is Government the Solution or the Problem? Its Purpose and Limits

Man's capacity for evil makes democracy necessary and man's capacity for good makes democracy possible.
—REINHOLD NIEBUHR

It is perfectly true that the government is best which governs least. It is equally true that the government is best which provides most.
—WALTER LIPPMANN

On January 12, 2010, a devastating earthquake centered near Port-au-Prince brought Haiti into the international spotlight. Computations of the final death toll varied widely, ranging from at least 50,000 to possibly more than 300,000 dead in the aftermath. Estimates of the economic damages suggest that the final cost will total between 7 and 13 billion dollars, earning the Haitian earthquake a place in the record books among the worst natural disasters ever to strike the Western Hemisphere.

The international response to the disaster was immediate. Billions of dollars in aid poured into Haiti, and more than 10,000 non-governmental organizations worked to alleviate the suffering.

By the one-year anniversary of the quake, however, almost a million people remained homeless, most of the rubble had yet to be cleared, and the majority of Haitians lacked permanent jobs. Why had so many organizations and so much aid apparently achieved so little?

The lack of a stable, well-functioning government was one significant barrier that hindered the ability of these groups to meet the desperate needs of the Haitian people. Insufficient roads, education, communication, and basic sanitation are among the many obstacles that made progress so difficult. Without these basic structures in place, it is extremely challenging to transport aid workers and supplies to where they are needed most. Government corruption and inefficiency make the problems even worse.

Already the poorest nation in the Western Hemisphere, the struggling nation was unprepared to respond to such a horrific natural disaster. The widespread poverty, homelessness, and despair in Haiti before and after the earthquake offer a powerful reminder of what can happen when government is too weak.

At the opposite end of the scale, the failed communist experiment in the former Soviet Union offers a stark example of the devastating effects of unchecked state power. Communist political systems, like that in the Soviet Union, outlawed all independent, non-communist organizations or groups. As a result, professional societies, unions, churches, youth groups, sports teams, and the like were under the direct control of the Communist party or had to meet illegally and at great personal risk to the participants. Because of this extensive repression, the only significant institutions in the Soviet Union were the state, the Communist party, and the family, with much overlap between the state and Communist party. The Soviet Union's all-consuming power led to massive state abuses that left an estimated 20 to 50 million people dead.

Looking back, it is not surprising that the downfall of communism began in Poland, the one Eastern European nation where independent organizations, such as the Catholic Church, had managed to maintain some degree of freedom. Unlike other nations in the Soviet bloc, communist Poland had a history of labor strikes that led to the formation of Solidarity, an independent labor union, in 1980. The Polish Communist government banned Solidarity, imprisoned all of its leaders, and declared martial law in 1981 in an attempt to curb the organization's power. But economic and political problems in Poland forced the government to end its ban and engage in negotiations with Solidarity by 1989. These talks led to elections and the eventual end of communist rule in Poland. The events in Poland influenced other Eastern European dissidents and contributed to the collapse of communism throughout the region.

After centuries of trial and error, we have come to something close to a consensus: a well-run government is vital for quality of life. We don't want to live in a place like Haiti, nor do we want to live in a place like the former Soviet Union. Too little government leads to chaos and entrenched poverty; too much government control leads to fear and oppression. The key to good government is finding the right balance between too weak and too strong.

In this chapter, we'll look at some of the vital components of good government and its role in ordering society, exploring questions about the purpose and limits of government. We'll also look briefly at two of the hallmarks of the American constitutional system designed to divide authority and distribute power—separation of powers and federalism. Let's begin with a reminder of a few important biblical themes that can guide our thoughts and actions toward government.

Government and Biblical Authority

Government is one of God's gifts to His creation. Like all human institutions in our fallen world, government is far from perfect, but it has essential purposes and functions that help us to survive and thrive. Paul's famous passage in Romans 13 reminds us that all authority is ultimately from God and therefore demands our honor and respect:

> *Let everyone be subject to the governing authorities, for there is no authority except that which God has established. The authorities that exist have been established by God. . . . Therefore, it is necessary to submit to the authorities, not only because of possible punishment but also as a matter of conscience. This is also why you pay taxes, for the authorities are God's servants, who give their full time to governing. Give to everyone what you owe them: If you owe taxes, pay taxes; if revenue, then revenue; if respect, then respect; if honor, then honor.* (Romans 13: 1, 5–7)

As followers of Christ, we are first under the authority of God and then under the authority of our government. Of course our allegiance to God must always come first, but we are called to submit to those in authority and pay our taxes.

HOW TO PRAY (AND HOW NOT TO PRAY) FOR THE PRESIDENT

★ ★ ★

LESS THAN A YEAR AFTER Barack Obama took the oath of office to serve as the 44th president, bumper stickers began to appear with the phrase, "Pray for Obama," followed by a reference to Psalm 109:8. What a powerful reminder that we are all called to pray for those in authority, right?

The verse accompanying the call to prayer suggests the slogan is actually more cruel than kind, for it reads: "May his days be few; may another take his place of leadership." The verses immediately following offer even stronger curses such as "may his children be fatherless and his wife a widow" (v. 9) and "may his descendants be cut off, their names blotted out from the next generation" (v. 13).

The call to prayer for our leaders is not a laughing matter; it is a command from God we should take seriously. It may be easier to pray for leaders that we voted for, but God calls us to pray for all of those in authority, regardless of our views on their policies and leadership.

The website of the Presidential Prayer Team (http://www.presidentialprayerteam.com) is one useful resource that can help guide our daily prayer for elected officials. You'll find daily prayers, weekly "featured leaders" from the three branches of government and the armed forces for whom to pray, highlights of the president's daily schedule, and other tools to help you follow the biblical command to lift governmental leaders to God in prayer.

In much the same way, we are told to pray for those who have authority over us: "I urge, then, first of all, that petitions, prayers, intercession and thanksgiving be made for all people—for kings and all those in authority, that we may live peaceful and quiet lives in all godliness and holiness. This is good, and pleases God our Savior" (1 Timothy 2:1–3). We are not told we have to agree with those in authority, but our Christian duty requires us to respect our political leaders and support them in prayer.

Key Components of Good Government

Properly functioning governments rely on mutual accountability. Governments and their citizens are accountable to one another, and all (whether they admit it or not) are ultimately accountable to God. A good and effective government creates a community of mutual accountability and responsibility where everyone gives and receives.

What Government Does for Us

What should we expect government to do for its people? One of the most important government functions is maintaining the "rule of law." Laws should reflect a concern for the general well-being of everyone and outline the responsibilities we have to one another as a part of a political community. As such, they create clear boundaries for how people can live and work together peacefully. Public safety officers help enforce the laws and maintain order. Government officials also help enforce law by creating guidelines to put laws into practice. Judges and courts support the law by providing a place to settle disagreements. These and other similar protections help create safe places for us to live and work.

★ ★ ★

A good and effective government creates a
community of mutual accountability and
responsibility where everyone gives and receives.

★ ★ ★

Government also provides "public goods"—those basic goods and services that are beneficial to many people, meet significant needs, and are available to everyone equally. Infrastructure such as roads, highways, and bridges; clean and safe drinking water; free schooling from kindergarten through high school; and police and fire protection are just a few examples. Indeed, most Americans are so accustomed to ready access to public goods and services that we give little thought to the ways in which government provides for our basic needs, public health, safety, and security. Government also helps sustain private institutions such as schools, churches, and families that are essential partners for building and maintaining a robust society.

Good government creates an environment in which most of its people will be able to thrive, but it also meets the basic needs of those who cannot care for themselves. Families, churches, and other community institutions have essential roles in caring for the needy. But these systems sometimes fail, and some problems and conditions are so deeply rooted in the structure of society that government is likely the last and best resource to address them. We call such services "safety-net" programs because they provide an ultimate layer of protection for the most vulnerable in society, such as children, people with disabilities, and the elderly.

Another essential component of a well-functioning government is access to "free markets," a term commonly used to describe the framework for private property and enterprise that allows businesses to prosper and innovate as they provide employment, goods, and services. At the same time, governments exercise the power to regulate, holding people and organizations accountable and establishing measures to safeguard citizens. While all modern democracies recognize the need for upholding both free markets and a regulatory state, nations differ significantly in how they strike this balance between these two essentials.

What Government Requires and Expects of Its People

Just as citizens benefit from the stability and resources government can provide, so do people need to do their part to help sustain a just society. Government expects citizens to care for themselves and their families, to respect the life and property of others, and to contribute generally to the collective good. Although most people do their part, others fail to live up to their responsibilities. In these instances, political leaders must decide how to respond. One answer is for government to compel certain actions, writing and enforcing laws that require everyone to act in certain ways. Over time, citizens of modern governments have grown accustomed to paying taxes to help support the work of government, observing traffic laws that maintain public safety, and following the criminal code designed to protect life and property. We comply and expect the same from others. Those who violate the law are subject to punishment.

Although many laws are clearly necessary to maintain a just society, we can and should debate the proper range and scope of governmental authority. Observers will disagree about which actions should be required and which should be voluntary. Too few laws lead to disorder and chaos; too many restrictions lead to oppression. Citizens can and should review the actions of governmental leaders to monitor potential abuses of power.

GLOBAL DIFFERENCES WITH LASTING CONSEQUENCES

★ ★ ★

What difference can government make? Every nation state has its own governing structures that have particular strengths, weaknesses, and distinguishing features. Some governments are more effective than others at meeting the needs of their people, but all are flawed and broken institutions.

Although there is no perfect formula that guarantees good governance, we can assess their relative success and failure by comparing different measures of quality of life. Consider a sampling of different indicators of health and education in three different countries: the East African nation of Zambia that ranks among the least developed nations in the world, the South American country of Ecuador that ranks near the middle, and the United States that ranks among the most developed nations.

	Zambia	Ecuador	United States
Life expectancy at birth	47.3	75.4	79.6
% of population undernourished	45	13	<5
Adult literacy rate	71.4	91	n/a
Average years of schooling	6.5	7.6	12.4
Internet users (per 100 people)	5.5	28.8	75.9

Source: United Nations Development Program, International Development Indicators; accessed at http://hdrstats.undp.org/en/countries.

Between Liberty and Tyranny:
The Structure of American Government

When a group of leaders met in Philadelphia, Pennsylvania, in 1787 to discuss government reform, those men we now call the "Founding Fathers" ended up creating a completely new governmental system based on the principles we have just discussed. At the time of the founding, most countries were ruled by all-powerful monarchs. The founders distrusted human nature and feared concentrating too much power in anyone's hands, so they designed a new system of government that offered a sharp break from the aristocratic tradition so common elsewhere. Concerned that individuals are selfish, they also believed that citizens needed to be kept in check. In crafting what we now know as the United States Constitution, they sought to balance two concerns: creating a government strong enough to meet the needs of the people but weak enough to preserve citizens' freedoms.

Their solution to this problem was to divide government power so that no one person or group could gain complete control. In so doing, the founders established a principle now known as separation of powers. We use this term to describe the division of authority among the three different branches of government: the legislative that makes the laws, the executive that implements and enforces them, and the judicial that interprets them. Each branch has some independent authority, but their powers overlap by design. We call this system checks and balances because the branches are forced to work together to accomplish many tasks, dispersing power further.

But dividing power between three branches of government is only one aspect of our limited government. Power is also separated by splitting authority between multiple layers of government, a system we call federalism. At the time they drafted the Constitution, the founders would have known only two systems of government—a unitary system in which a single central government had all the political authority and a confederal system that gave ultimate power to states or provinces. Instead, they designed a new hybrid, a federal system that balances and divides power between the national government and the sovereign states. The national (or federal) government has certain roles and responsibilities that govern the entire country, but the states also have their own independent powers, functions, and laws. Citizens thus owe allegiance to both the state and national governments and must abide by both sets of laws. We'll examine these features of the system in more detail in the next chapter.

As we have seen, the government created in the Constitution was carefully designed to separate and diversify government power. Because no single individual, group, or level or branch of government wields much independent control, the founders believed they created the right combination of a government that was neither too strong nor too weak.

On the Outside Looking In: Christians and Government

As we have seen, a robust but limited government is necessary to seek justice and provide for the common good. But we also must consider how Christians should interact with government.

As part of a political community, we can and should pay attention to what elected officials are doing and speak out when government appears to veer off course. But we need to do so while still showing respect for those in authority and the offices they hold. Unfair criticisms and belittling talk can cause us to lose trust in the very people and institutions at the heart of American democracy. Some critiques seem less about holding elected officials to account and more about making fun of politicians and the causes they support. Many blogs, talk shows, and other forms of political commentary are quick to attack elected officials, heaping criticism on their proposals and mocking their blunders and missteps. As Christians seeking to honor God, we should choose a different tone, respectfully raising important questions about policy proposals based on facts and careful arguments.

When evaluating political proposals, it is very tempting to ask how they will likely affect us, weighing what we stand to gain or lose personally. As kingdom citizens, however, we should think less about self and more about others, assessing how particular proposals might help or hurt the most vulnerable in society. We need to move from thinking primarily about how government appears to help or harm our individual interests, instead considering more broadly how government can help secure the common good.

At the same time, we also need to recognize and accept the limits of government. If a problem is easy to solve, politicians have already found a solution and put it into practice. The issues that remain on the political agenda are therefore the most complex problems that likely do not have simple, straightforward solutions.

★ ★ ★

In their zeal for what is right and true, some Christians blur the distinctions between the kingdom of God and the kingdom of man.

★ ★ ★

With this in mind, if we think government might be best able to address an issue, we should start by asking two questions. First, we need to ask: "Is this a problem government should help address?" As we have seen in this chapter, certain categories of issues seem a natural fit for public policy. In general, we think of law regulating those areas of life that affect the public good, leaving individuals otherwise free to live their lives as they choose. A second question follows from the first: "Is this a problem government can help address?" Government seeks to order society through a combination of demanding some things of its citizens, forbidding others, and taking deliberate actions. We need to determine which actions are possible to regulate and which are not. Laws cannot change hearts and minds, so we shouldn't expect them to do so.

Unfortunately, many people look to the political process to solve problems that it has no ability to address. In their zeal for what is right and true, some Christians blur the distinctions between the kingdom of God and the kingdom of man. As the late Congressman Paul Henry observed:

> Nothing is so frustrating to me as a public official as to hear the clergy decry the "decline of values in our society," and turn to the Congress for social salvation! The role of government—at least in a constitutional system—is not that of "making new men," but addressing the conflicts between them. Government is not responsible for the human condition, it responds to it.[1]

We need to approach politics aware of the strengths and limits of democratic government, not expecting more from the political process than it can deliver.

Finding the Best Balance

As we have seen, the best government is a balanced one—it should be stronger than that in Haiti, but it should be weaker than the authoritarian state that created such despair in the former Soviet Union. Government needs to provide the fundamental institutions and infrastructure to meet its citizens' basic needs and allow them to flourish, but it should not seek such tight control that it takes away fundamental freedoms and crushes the human spirit.

These first three chapters introduced ideas and concepts to help begin our discussion. The next two sections of this book will give you tools to help you approach politics first and foremost as a follower of Christ. With these introductory thoughts behind us, we are ready to look at how our political system works in practice.

Our next stop is a quick overview of local, state, and national government, showing you who is in charge of what and why it matters.

QUESTIONS FOR DISCUSSION

Reflecting

1. What are some of the potential dangers of government wielding too much power? What are some of the potential dangers of a
government that is too weak?

2. In what ways do you depend on government in your daily life?
How do government services, laws, and protections make your
life better, and how might they create problems?

Responding

3. What are some things that government can likely do better than
any other institution? What are some issues and problems that
government likely cannot address? What are some practical ways
you can support the government's work, and what are some ways
you can help address issues and problems that government cannot?

PART 2

★ ★ ★

Government in Action: How Our System Works

Chapter 4

★ ★ ★

Who Runs the Show? The Roles of Local, State, and Federal Government

We are all imperfect. We cannot expect a perfect government.

—WILLIAM HOWARD TAFT

The seven thousand–person town of Orland Hills, Illinois, does not have a public library, but they have a five-person library board. The Richmond Township Cemetery District has three board members to oversee four cemeteries. The two commissioners for the Lincoln-Lansing Drainage District in the southern Chicago suburbs each earn a mere $75 a year to keep twenty miles of ditches clean, yet the drainage district spends about $3,000 annually to bill homeowners for their services.[1]

In contrast, the sprawling county of Cook County, Illinois, is the nineteenth largest unit of government in the United States. The Cook County Board President and the seventeen commissioners serve 5.2 million residents and control an annual budget of more than $3 billion. The county includes 128 cities, villages, and towns and employs more than 23,000 full-time personnel.[2]

These are just four of the 8,500 units of government in Illinois, which range from tiny taxing districts with seemingly meager duties to a county with a population larger than that of 29 states. The wide diversity in size and scope of local governments in Illinois highlights important questions. Does a single state need that many governing units? When is government too large, and when is it too small? As we saw in Chapter 3, modern societies need well-functioning government to develop and thrive. We elect people to serve in a range of capacities to deliver public services and provide for the common good. We want our elected officials to be close enough to the communities they serve that they are aware of and responsible to local needs and concerns. But we also expect efficiency and cost-effectiveness.

GOVERNMENT ALL AROUND US

★ ★ ★

IN DAILY LIFE, we interact with the various levels of government without giving much thought to its federal structure. Consider just a few of the many ways we each rely on multiple levels of government in just the first few minutes of a typical day. Climbing out of bed, you turn on the lights and other electrical devices, likely giving little thought to your dependence on public utilities. You stumble into a shower of warm water connected to your home by the city water and sewer department. As you hurry to work, you heed local traffic laws that help you safely maneuver a system of roads maintained by a combination of city, county, state, and national governments. You stop for a quick cup of coffee from a local restaurant regularly inspected by the county health department and order a quick breakfast made with ingredients deemed safe by the United States Department of Agriculture.

The American system includes multiple layers of government with components that range widely in size and scope. This structure helps limit the reach of government by drawing some power away from Washington and sharing it with governments in each state. States are free to differ from one another, yet they share many of the same goals. Let's look at the different levels of government in the United States and the ways in which they complement and compete with one another.

The Three Branches of the National Government

Debates about the proper role and reach of government often focus on the actions of the elected officials who capture most of the attention of the news media: the president, members of Congress, and the justices on the Supreme Court. Since many conversations about government begin with reflections on what is happening in Washington, D.C., we will begin our discussion there, considering each of the three branches of the national government to see how they work. We'll turn first to where laws originate, the legislative branch.

The Lawmakers: The Legislative Branch

The framers expected Congress, the primary lawmaking institution of the national government, to wield the most power, so they divided it into two chambers: the House of Representatives and the Senate.

Elected to two-year terms to represent districts of roughly equal size, members of the House are expected to be the closest to the people and their local concerns. Each of the 435 members represents about 700,000 people. Given its large membership, the House is governed by strict rules that help limit and shape debate, and party leaders try to exercise tight control over their delegations.

THE PROBLEM WITH WORDS:
WHAT IS THE FEDERAL GOVERNMENT?

★ ★ ★

WHEN MOST AMERICANS talk about the government in Washington, they use the phrase "federal government." When political scientists describe the system of government created in the Constitution, they say it is a "federal" system. Using the same words in two different but related contexts can lead to confusion. To try and minimize confusion as you read this chapter, I will use the term "national government" to refer to those institutions and structures that govern the United States.

The other chamber of Congress, the Senate, includes two members from each state elected to six-year terms. With their longer terms and larger constituencies, senators are more distant from the people and thus freer to concern themselves with the national interest. The Constitution grants a few powers to the Senate alone; these include offering advice and consent on presidential appointments and voting on approval of treaties.

The Senate follows the tradition of unlimited debate, which means in practice that its members can speak on the floor of the chamber as long as they please. When senators delay or stop legislation with unlimited debate, we call this practice a filibuster. A vote from sixty or more senators invokes cloture, a practice used to cut off debate and force a measure to the floor. Because of these practices, the Senate needs the cooperation of at least sixty members to do most of its business, so neither political party has held a true working majority in recent decades.

Traditional legislation requires cooperation between the two chambers of Congress. For a bill to become a law, the proposal must pass in the House and the Senate in identical form before going to the president for a signature. When you take into account that many bills are hundreds of pages long, one wonders how both chambers ever reach agreement on every single word.[3]

Congressional Powers

Article I of the Constitution lists several congressional powers including taxation, borrowing money, regulating interstate commerce, coining money, creating courts, and declaring war. Congress, and only Congress, holds the power of the purse; that is, its members decide how to spend all federal dollars. The president has a role in the budget process, but members of Congress make the final decisions. Legislators also have significant (though shared) authority over economic, foreign, and domestic policy.

Congress was not a dominating force in national government for much of American history. The state of New York, for example, had a larger budget than that of the United States for most of the nineteenth century. As the size and scope of national needs grew, so did the role of Congress. Although Article I, Section 8 specifies particular congressional powers in sixteen clauses, the section ends with what has become known as the elastic clause, which empowers Congress "to make all Laws which shall be necessary and proper for carrying into Execution the foregoing Powers, and all other Powers vested by this Constitution in the Government of the United States, or any Department or Officer thereof." Supreme Court decisions interpreted this and other clauses in ways that expanded the scope of congressional powers, so Congress can now enact legislation on a broad range of policies.

The Enforcers: The Executive Branch

A second branch of government, the executive, includes its formal head, the president, and the several million individuals who work as part of the federal bureaucracy to enforce and administer the laws. Although the framers left some room for the office to expand through the years, the presidency is an office of delegated powers. Ultimately, all presidential power comes from two sources—the Constitution and the laws—so the president has no independent base of power.

Article II, what early twentieth century scholar Edward S. Corwin famously described as the "most loosely drawn chapter of the Constitution,"[4] establishes the American presidency. Section 1 creates the office: "The executive power shall be vested in a President of the United States of America." Section 2 bestows national security powers, stating that the president "shall be Commander in Chief of the Army and Navy." A vague statement in Section 3, often called the "take-care clause," gives the power to "take care that the laws are faithfully executed." Over time, presidents have used this clause to justify broadening their powers.

The Constitution delineates a few other areas of presidential authority. As the nation's chief diplomat, the president nominates and receives ambassadors and makes treaties (subject to Senate approval). Control over legislation is limited; presidents can recommend (but not introduce) legislation, report to Congress, convene special legislative sessions, and attempt to prevent bills from becoming law with a veto. The president nominates high-level executive branch officials and all members of the federal judiciary, but all such nominations require Senate approval.

Executive Branch Powers

Even though we look to the president as the symbol of executive power, in reality the president is just the highest-ranking person leading a multilayered bureaucracy. Immediately below the president are about 3,000 political appointees. Under them are roughly 2.7 million executive branch employees and another 2 million workers in the Defense Department. Almost all members of the executive branch are civil servants, employees chosen and promoted based on merit, not political connections. As presidential administrations and their political appointees come and go, the workers at the heart of the bureaucracy remain, providing continuity for government and wielding considerable power.

Although we typically don't think of government bureaucracy as a major power center, in actuality executive branch officials make decisions on a daily basis that directly affect our lives. Once Congress passes a bill and the president signs it into law, members of the executive branch decide whether and how to implement it, writing and enforcing the codes and regulations that will determine how the law applies and whom it affects.

The Interpreters: The Judicial Branch

The legislative branch writes the law and the executive enforces it, but one more essential power remains. The judicial branch interprets the law, deciding whether laws and the means of enforcing them are constitutional.

Article III of the Constitution gives very little detail about federal courts, merely stating that "the judicial power of the United States shall be vested in one supreme Court, and in such Inferior courts as the Congress may from time to time ordain and establish." Congress moved quickly to fulfill this duty, creating a three-tiered federal court system in the Judiciary Act of 1789.

Judges have greatly expanded the power and role of the federal courts through their own rulings. In actions that culminated in the 1803 case *Marbury v. Madison*, the Supreme Court established the power of judicial review, the right of the courts to evaluate and potentially overturn actions of other branches of government or states. If the justices find that a law violates the Constitution, they throw it out. Legislators have few options if the Court invalidates a law; their best hope is rewriting the statute with changes likely to address the justices' concerns.

Although we typically don't think of government bureaucracy as a major power center, in actuality executive branch officials make decisions on a daily basis that directly affect our lives.

Like other high-level appointments, the president selects and the Senate confirms judicial appointees, but unlike other positions in government, judges serve "during good behavior." In practice, this means they have lifetime appointments designed to insulate them from politics and public opinion.

Federal judges decide cases involving federal laws, treaties, or the Constitution, and some of the cases involving citizens of more than one state. The lowest level, or trial courts, in the federal system are called district courts. Above these are the U.S. Courts of Appeal, and above them is the Supreme Court.

The Supreme Court and Its Powers

The nine Supreme Court justices consider about 8,000 cases each year, agreeing to hear between 70 and 90 of them. Almost all of these cases reach the Court on appeal. If a party on one side of a case does not agree with a lower court's ruling, they may request a writ of certiorari, a formal petition asking the Court to review their case. Justices agree to hear those cases they believe have the most legal significance.

THEORY MEETS PRACTICE: PREDICTING HOW JUDGES MIGHT RULE

★ ★ ★

EACH TIME THE PRESIDENT seeks to fill a vacancy on the Supreme Court, observers try to predict how the new justice will rule on important cases. We wonder: How will the nominee decide cases that come before the Court? To what extent might personal or political beliefs affect the outcomes? Although there are no simple answers to such complicated questions, most justices are rather consistent in their approach to their work. If you know a nominee's judicial philosophy you can often predict how he or she will decide future cases.

All judges have a judicial philosophy, a view of what role the courts should play. Those who advocate *judicial restraint* believe that the court should avoid overturning previous decisions if at all possible. In addition, since judges are unelected, the court should defer to legislative decisions whenever possible. On the other hand, proponents of *judicial activism* advocate a more proactive role for the court. At times, they argue, it is necessary for the court to overturn a law, reject a presidential action, or go beyond the specific words of the Constitution to address contemporary issues.

Although many people would like Supreme Court justices to advocate particular public policies in their rulings, this is not the Court's primary role. The Court's opinions set precedent for all other courts in the United States, so the justices want to create standards that other judges can apply in similar cases. To accomplish this goal, justices sometimes create legal "tests," criteria other judges can use to determine if a statute under review violates the Constitution. In the case *Miller v. California*, for example, the court had to decide if the First Amendment freedom of speech included obscenity. Ruling that states could indeed restrict obscene speech, they created a test to help judges and legislators differentiate between obscene and legitimate speech. One part of the test, called the LAPS test, asks if the content has literary, artistic, political, or scientific value. According to this test, an image of a nude human figure in an anatomy textbook would have scientific value and thus count as protected free speech, whereas the same image on a billboard might be classified as obscenity that government could restrict.

The Other Layers of Government

Now that we have looked briefly at the three branches of the national government, let's look at the other layers of government in the United States.

State Government 101: Fifty Different Designs

One of the hallmarks of a federal system is that it allows states flexibility to design their governments as they choose. Most state governments resemble each other in many ways, but no two systems are exactly alike. If you wonder about how a particular aspect of state or local government works, the answer is frustratingly simple: it depends on the state. Most questions will have fifty different answers.

Each state has its own governing structure established by its state constitution. Although the organization of state governments varies widely, all states mirror the national system in that they divide power between executive, legislative, and judicial authorities. All states elect a governor to oversee executive functions, but they differ in the number and types of other officials elected statewide to executive offices.

All states have some form of state legislature to craft state laws; forty-nine states divide legislative power into two elected chambers much like Congress. The lone exception, Nebraska, changed to a single chamber, or unicameral, legislature in 1937. Much like their congressional counterparts, state legislators are in control of the budgetary purse strings. Governors can sign or veto pending state laws, acting as a check on state lawmakers.

Each state also has its own system of courts to interpret state law, manage disputes, and enforce criminal codes. Some states hold elections for all or most judges, others have a system for appointing judges, and a few fill judicial posts by a combination of the two. State court systems are incredibly busy, managing 95 percent of the legal cases in the United States. In 2008, for example, approximately 15 million complete civil cases and almost 13 million complete criminal cases were filed in state courts across the nation.[5]

Almost all criminal codes are state laws, so state and local governments devote significant resources for investigating crimes and prosecuting and punishing offenders. Police officers, sheriff deputies, prosecutors, public defenders, and probation officers are just a few examples of the state and local government employees needed to maintain law and order.

Local Government

Each state's constitution and laws create and authorize a particular system of local government. Some state constitutions allow for home rule, a mechanism to permit local areas to govern themselves, but all states retain ultimate authority over the governing structures they create. Most states are partitioned into counties that are further divided into municipalities. Municipalities such as cities, towns, and villages are usually arranged around a population center and provide a range of services designed to meet citizens' daily needs. Fire and police protection, parks and recreation, and public works such as streets and roads are among their central tasks.

Like their state and national counterparts, many county and municipal governments also have executive, legislative, and judicial functions. For example, most cities and larger towns entrust the executive function to an elected mayor, an appointed city manager who oversees the daily operations, or a combination of the two. Many cities and towns have an elected council that serves a legislative function and other boards who oversee libraries, planning and zoning, parks and recreation, and the like. Each state also has a system of local governing units that cross municipal boundaries to oversee public agencies such as school districts and water authorities.

Forced to Work Together: Layers of Government in Action

As we have seen, the Constitution established several mechanisms to divide and limit government power. A practical example can help you see how the different levels and branches of government share responsibility for policy. Consider the current political debate over abortion. Which branches and levels of government have the most influence over abortion policy? As we will see, the answer to this seemingly simple question is quite complex.

Who Has Power over Abortion Law?

Because states retain the power to write and enforce most criminal laws, state legislatures determined abortion laws for most of American history. Each state had freedom to allow doctors to perform abortions, to regulate the practice, or to forbid abortion entirely.

The balance of power on this issue changed in 1973 with the Supreme Court ruling commonly known as *Roe v. Wade.* (See the sidebar, "What Really Happened in *Roe v. Wade?*" for more details on the Court's opinion.) In its decision, the Supreme Court ruled that many forms of abortion restrictions violated the Constitution and were therefore invalid. The Court's action was a potent check on the power of state legislatures, setting new boundaries for what kinds of laws they could and could not enforce. This action also changed the balance and focus of the abortion debate from the states to the Supreme Court.

Once abortion was no longer an issue primarily addressed by state governments, officials in national politics entered the debate. Presidential candidates began talking about the issue, campaigning in support of pro-life or pro-choice policies even though the president has very little independent power to affect abortion policy. Past presidents have issued executive orders permitting or forbidding federal funding of abortion services and abortion counseling, for example, but they do not have the power to change the legal status of abortion. Presidents can exert important indirect influence on the policy debate, however, through their power to nominate Supreme Court justices.

Members of Congress have also entered the debate, looking for ways they can influence abortion policy. Like presidents, they find few venues for directly influencing abortion law. Senators have some influence in the judicial confirmation process, for they can approve or deny a president's judicial nominee. Congress has little hope of passing legislation that would either prohibit or guarantee national access to abortion because the principle of federalism severely limits congressional power over criminal law. In practice, Congress is limited to small and symbolic actions on this issue.

WHAT REALLY HAPPENED IN *ROE V. WADE*?

★ ★ ★

IN THE LANDMARK decision of *Roe v. Wade*, the Court answered the legal question: Does the Constitution guarantee a right to privacy? In a 7-2 decision, the justices ruled that the Constitution implicitly guarantees the right to privacy and that this right includes abortion. Privacy rights are not absolute, however, so states must balance them with their legitimate interest in protecting the potentiality of human life.

The opinion established a system of enforcement, ruling that states must leave the abortion decision to a woman and her physician in the first three months of pregnancy. As the pregnancy progresses, however, states could begin to restrict abortion, regulating the procedure during the second trimester of pregnancy if the laws relate to maternal health. After the point of viability when the fetus could survive outside the womb, states could regulate or even forbid abortion, except in cases when it would preserve the life or health of the mother.

In later cases, the Supreme Court has refined its stance on abortion law, gradually permitting states more room to change abortion laws. According to the standards in effect since the 1992 decision *Planned Parenthood v. Casey*, states can prohibit elective abortions after actual viability, and states can regulate abortion before this point as long as any restrictions meet an "undue burden" standard. According to this legal test, allowable restrictions must not present a "substantial obstacle" to obtaining an abortion.

State legislatures still have some power to write and enforce abortion regulations, but their statutes must not conflict with the guidelines set in Supreme Court rulings. If the Court were to overturn *Roe v. Wade*, the balance of power would shift from the Supreme Court back to state legislatures, and each state would once again have power to forbid, regulate, or permit abortion as they chose. Of course, both sides in the abortion debate tend to forget or overlook this, failing to acknowledge that overturning *Roe* would not instantly change abortion law.

As the abortion example demonstrates, the different institutions of the state and national governments share power over public policy, and the balance of power shifts over time. When seeking policy change, recall the principles of separation of powers and federalism to keep your expectations realistic and to guide you to which level or branch of government has the most power over a particular issue.

The Slow and Humble Road

The founders designed American government to control and disperse power, and they clearly succeeded. Sociologist William Martin explains their reasoning this way:

> The system of checks and balances they built into the Constitution was informed not only by the recognition that good citizens may differ over the proper course of action, but also, at least in part, by the biblical understanding of humans as fallible and prone to wrongdoing and therefore frequently in need of some healthy opposition from their fellows. Nobody, in their view, has a corner on Truth, Justice, and the American Way.[6]

The dispersion of power in American government makes quick and sweeping change almost impossible, but these safeguards also protect us. Political change takes time, and the multilayered system makes room for many voices to enter the discussion and help shape the outcomes. Although the complexity and limits of the system can frustrate legitimate desires to make a difference, the design of our system can also encourage us to approach politics with patience and humility.

★ ★ ★

The dispersion of power in American government makes quick and sweeping change almost impossible, but these safeguards also protect us.

★ ★ ★

Now that we have looked at the basic structure and institutions of American government, let's turn our discussion to some of the tools that help individuals interact with government. In particular, we will look at ways that political ideology can shape our understanding of government and we will consider some of the strengths and weaknesses of political parties.

QUESTIONS FOR DISCUSSION

Reflecting

1. In your opinion, which of the three branches of the federal government—executive, legislative, or judicial—has the most influence over the lives of everyday Americans? Explain.

2. What types of government policies and programs are best handled by the national government? Which are best handled by state and local governments?

Responding

3. In what ways can learning more about the roles and functions of different aspects of government help you be a better citizen?

Chapter 5

★ ★ ★

Left, Right, or Center: Party, Ideology, and Politics

What is a Democrat? One who believes that Republicans have ruined the country. What is a Republican? One who believes that the Democrats would ruin the country.

—AMBROSE BIERCE

When you are pulling people out of the water and off of rooftops, there are no Republicans and no Democrats.

—CHARLIE MELANCON

Democrats: The Party of Reason. Republicans: The Party of Treason." "Hate. Lies. Greed. The Republican Way." "Obama Reid Pelosi. The Axis of Idiots." "lib·er·al: noun: A person so open-minded their brains have fallen out." So read some of the more outrageous slogans for political bumper stickers, coffee mugs, and T-shirts you can find online. Although we would not accept such cruel comments targeted toward most groups in society, some staunch partisans seem to think nothing of speaking so viciously about their political opponents. What is it about politics that can bring out such fury? Must political differences turn us into enemies?

In this chapter, we'll look at the variety of political perspectives common in the United States, considering important ways that ideology and parties shape our views and actions. After describing the core beliefs of the American political "left," "right," and "center," we'll look at some ways political parties help make our political system work and other ways they might steer us off course.

Political Ideology in the United States

In chapter 2 we talked briefly about political identity, noting that political belief systems are very important for many people. The technical term for such convictions is political ideology, those values and beliefs about government that provide a framework for thinking about politics. In theory, ideology is consistent and stable; a person's views hold together tightly and coherently, remaining about the same for a lifetime. In reality, however, most of our belief systems are not quite so well-defined. Some people discover that their political views change over time. Others may hold consistently conservative or liberal views about many issues yet seem to have haphazard or contradictory perspectives on others. Many of us may not know much or care deeply about every issue that governments might address.

The two most common ideologies in contemporary American politics are usually labeled liberalism and conservatism. As we will see, these variant perspectives differ in their emphasis on liberty or equality and in their views on the role of government in society.

On the Right: Conservatives and Republicans

The strictest definition of the term suggests that conservatives hope to "conserve" things as they are, wanting to preserve tradition and supporting gradual change only when necessary. Conservatives emphasize individual rights and responsibilities. Holding a more pessimistic view of human nature, they are likely to view government as a necessary evil to preserve law and order. From this viewpoint, government best serves the people by restraining evil, protecting citizens, and providing laws and moral codes that serve as a foundation for society. Otherwise, government should leave the people free to make their own choices. If individuals make poor decisions, they must accept the consequences.

Conservatives are often suspicious of government trying to do too much, raising concerns about government policies that might interfere with business and hurt the economy. Believing government decision making should be as close to the people as possible to protect their freedom, conservatives usually prefer that state and local officials have more control than leaders in Washington. Traditionally the party of business, tax cuts, law and order, and a strong defense, the Republican party is the most natural home for conservatives in the United States.

To the political right of conservatism is libertarianism, a political philosophy that opposes almost all government restrictions. Libertarians emphasize individual freedom, maintaining that each person should have the liberty to do anything that does not take away the liberty of others. A traditional libertarian would disagree with government regulations they see as limiting individual freedom, be they laws that affect businesses such as clean air standards or laws that affect individuals like regulation of narcotics.

On the Left: Liberals and Democrats

Liberals emphasize community and equality, typically holding a more positive view of government than conservatives. This viewpoint argues that individuals on their own cannot be expected to act in ways that serve the common good, so government is necessary to promote equality and justice. Believing that government is a positive institution that makes way for change and progress, liberals look to government to address structural and institutional problems in society, problems they contend will not go away without government help.

A NEW KIND OF CONSERVATIVE?
THE RISE OF THE TEA PARTY

★ ★ ★

IN THE MONTHS leading into the 2010 federal elections, a new political movement gained strength in American politics. Taking their name in part from the Boston Tea Party protests against the British colonial government in 1773, a loose affiliation of grassroots activists across the country organized a range of advocacy efforts under the umbrella term "Tea Party."

Animated by the perception that government debt and deficits are growing out of control, these activists typically call for significant cuts in taxes and spending and argue for a return to the original meaning of the Constitution. Many Tea Party adherents are suspicious of the concentration of power, so they are more likely to work in loose affiliations of activists across the country than as part of a structured organization like the major political parties.

Tea Party activists were successful in helping shape political debate in the 2010 election. Several candidates who received Tea Party support won victories in Republican primaries, typically ousting candidates whose views were more in line with the mainstream party. About one third of the candidates in the 2010 general election who earned some form of Tea Party endorsement won elected office.

Liberals are likely to support public policies and programs that meet essential needs such as education, health care, and housing.

Concerned that unchecked free enterprise may increase inequality, liberals are likely to favor business regulations designed to protect workers, civil rights, and the environment. Given its history of implementing broad-based government programs, the Democratic party is the natural home for most liberals.

In recent years, the term "liberal" has become more politically charged. Conservative candidates and media personalities have found great success demonizing the term, so many left-leaning politicians now try to avoid it. Because of their ideological emphasis on progress, some traditional liberals prefer the label "progressive" as a better descriptor of their views.

To the political left of liberals are socialists who advocate greater redistribution of wealth and increased government control of the economy. In contrast to liberals who advocate working within the market economy, socialists believe that the means of production should be under community or government ownership and control.

In the Middle: Moderates and Independents

Although not an ideology in the technical sense of the term, some elected officials and many voters are centrists or moderates; that is, their view of government and political issues tends to be in between that of conservatives and liberals. In recent decades, the number of American voters who describe their political views as moderate has increased sharply.

Most people are political moderates for one of two reasons. They look for a "middle way" in politics, trying to find a balance between conservative and liberal proposals. Others may describe themselves as moderates because their views alternate between conservative and liberal, depending on the issue and defying simple ideological categories.

Many political centrists are uncomfortable identifying themselves as Democrats or Republicans, preferring instead to say they are independent of party. In practice, however, most Independents tend to vote rather consistently for the same party from election to election. About 4 of 10 Americans describe themselves as Independent.

Following the command to love God and neighbor, we should exercise great caution when using simple labels to describe complex ideas.

The Limits of Labels

Ideological labels can be helpful for understanding basic differences between political perspectives, but, like so many other ways that people tend to categorize and stereotype, such descriptors have only limited usefulness. Because terms like conservative and liberal describe a complex and diverse set of ideas, it is easy to distort and obscure their meaning. Particularly in the midst of heated political debate, some will use ideological labels as verbal weapons, attempting to discredit an opponent with a dismissive turn of phrase. Following the command to love God and neighbor, we should exercise great caution when using simple labels to describe complex ideas.

From Ideas to Actions: The Work of Political Parties

Most Americans connect their ideological views with one of the two major American political parties, the Democrats or the Republicans. Parties are an important element of the political process because their goal is helping candidates win office so they can shape public policy. Not content just to tell people what to think about politics, parties want to govern.

An interesting feature of American political parties is that they are completely voluntary. Anyone can claim to be a Republican, just as anyone can claim to be a Democrat. If you decide you don't like one party anymore, you can switch to another party at any time. Although party organizations can choose which candidates they want to help in campaigns, they have no direct control over individuals who claim their label. Consider the example of white supremacist and former Ku Klux Klan leader David Duke. He began his political career in Louisiana seeking office as a Democrat and eventually won a seat in the state legislature as a Republican. Neither party was eager to be connected with Duke and his controversial views, but nothing could stop him from running for office as a Democrat or as a Republican.

How Parties Make Elections Simpler

Even though most voters will never see their behind-the-scenes work or realize its importance, parties are central to the election process. As soon as the results of an election are announced, party organizations begin their work preparing for the next one. The first step is recruiting and training strong candidates. Although anyone can decide to run for political office, it is much easier to do so with the support of party activists.

Political parties help candidates prepare for elections in many ways. Perhaps most importantly, they help candidates raise money and energize voters. Even seemingly small races such as those for local office can cost tens of thousands of dollars, so fundraising is crucial for any campaign. Parties solicit their own donations that can indirectly help candidates, and they connect likely donors to candidates, helping fill their campaign bank accounts.

Political parties also help simplify elections. Most elections in the United States occur in two stages. First, the parties hold primary elections, conventions, or caucuses to select one person from a list of candidates who will represent the party. In the second stage, the general election, voters choose from lists of one candidate per party, and the person who wins the most votes assumes office. Ballots that list candidates with party labels help voters choose. Even if you know nothing else about a candidate except his or her party affiliation, the party label gives you important clues about the candidate's political views and priorities.

In addition to the practical ways parties participate in elections, they can also serve to unify voters. Parties bring voters together, building broad coalitions of supporters who have the power to make a difference.

How Parties Affect the Work of Government

Elections are a means for political parties to achieve their fundamental purpose—making public policy. Once parties succeed in getting their candidates elected, they serve an additional function, managing government institutions.

First and foremost, parties help organize government so it works more effectively. A single individual can do very little in government all alone, but groups of people can accomplish quite a bit. Knowing this law of practical politics, fellow partisans work together to coordinate government activities and achieve their policy goals.

Party leaders also work to influence elected officials, using a combination of rewards and punishments to encourage them to vote the party line. Some elected officials will do as their party leaders suggest, but all are free to ignore the efforts to pressure them. Party leaders walk a careful line, trying to promote Republican or Democratic unity without angering the rank and file too much. Because partisan identity is ultimately an individual's choice, elected officials can change party at any time. Senate Republicans saw this danger realized in April 2009, when then-Senator Arlen Specter switched from the Republican party to the Democratic party. With this move, Senate Democrats gained the crucial sixty votes they needed to push forward proposals Republicans were trying to block. In addition to organizing government, parties also work to turn election victories into policy. If you listen to the political analysis in the days following most federal elections, pundits will likely discuss who has a "mandate" from the people to implement new policies. Although analysis of polling data rarely reveals evidence to support such posturing, politicians nonetheless act as if the voters speak collectively through elections in support of particular issue positions. If partisan control of the presidency, the House, or the Senate changes from one party to the other, leaders usually interpret the result as a demand for change.

At the same time that the party in power tries to carry out its agenda, the other party serves as the "loyal opposition," proposing alternative policies, critiquing the current policy agenda, or somehow mixing the two. Members of the minority party look ahead to the next election with the hopes of regaining power.

BIPARTISAN ISN'T A BAD WORD

★ ★ ★

PERHAPS IT IS A sign of the times, but a common error I detect in early sessions of many of my classes is that students criticize elected officials for being too "bipartisan." Unknowingly, they confuse the term *partisanship*, fervent devotion to one party, with *bipartisanship*, working together across party lines. Maybe this confusion stems in part from their experiences. Displays of hyper-partisanship and political gridlock abound at almost all levels of government; contemporary American politics offers few examples of genuine bipartisanship and cooperation.

Measuring Partisanship

Although we cannot quantify partisanship, we can estimate the influence of parties on congressional activity. By almost all the measures political scientists have developed, party has a strong hold on members of Congress.

One way we measure the influence of party is to see how often the average legislator votes with his or her party. Recent data on party voting are striking indeed: members of Congress now vote with their party almost nine times out of ten, indicating that very few of them act independently of party leaders. Congressional scholar Barbara Sinclair looked at other places where party might affect legislative behavior, measuring the influence of party in committee action, the floor process, and presidential/congressional agreement on legislation. She found consistent patterns of partisanship in every arena.[1]

In the past three decades, the ideological divide between elected officials from both parties has widened substantially.

★ ★ ★

Another way to measure partisanship is to look at the range of ideological views within each party. When legislators in each party hold a wide array of views, they are more likely to work with colleagues across the party aisle. On the other hand, the fewer moderates in each party, the greater the distance between them and the smaller the likelihood of cooperation. In the past three decades, the ideological divide between elected officials from both parties has widened substantially. Almost all Republicans in Congress are conservative, almost all Democrats in Congress are liberal, and the number of moderates in both parties has declined sharply.

Such partisan patterns can lead to stalemate. At a time when party control of the House and Senate has been changing back and forth frequently between Democrats and Republicans, party leaders increase the pressure on legislators to toe the party line. The party currently in control wants to claim all major policy victories for itself and not risk sharing credit with its rivals. In turn, the party out of power doesn't want to help the other party do anything that might help them in the next election. In this highly charged environment, members of Congress may work across party lines to pass simple, non-controversial legislation, but they are less willing to work together on much else.

Ironically, at the same time that the ideological differences between elected officials are widening, voters' ties to political parties are weakening. The percentage of independent voters has grown so much that more people say they are independent of either party than define themselves as Republicans or Democrats. Even those voters attached to a particular party are typically more ideologically moderate than the elected officials who represent them.

The Perils of Partisanship

As we have seen, parties enhance the political process and contribute to a vibrant democracy in many positive ways. But they can do more harm than good if their leaders and devotees lose sight of the purpose, function, and limits of parties. Identification with a political party can be a very good thing, but excessive devotion to party creates many problems.

ONE STATE, TWO STATE: RED STATE, BLUE STATE

★ ★ ★

JOURNALISTS AND POLITICAL pundits like to talk about red and blue America, terms that refer to the giant election maps projected by the news media on Election Day to show which party's candidate has won in each state. "Red" states elected Republicans, and "blue" states chose Democrats.

Such color-coded maps reveal some interesting patterns, but they are not the most accurate portrayal of the depth of partisan attachments across the country. It is likely much more accurate to describe most states as "purple"—both Republican and Democrat at the same time.

Concerned by the messages communicated in simple red and blue electoral maps, Princeton professor Robert Vanderbei has created new election maps that use 256 shades of red and blue to distinguish the percentage of votes for each candidate. Counties where the Republican candidate won by a large majority were a vibrant red, those with strong Democratic wins were a vibrant blue, and areas with much closer margins became shades of purple. When displayed with these refinements, the new national map displays many shades of purple, showing an electorate that is closely divided between the two major parties in almost every state and region.[2]

Extreme partisanship can lead some people to an overly simplistic and unrealistic perspective on politics, acting as if each political question has only two sides, a stock Republican and an obvious Democratic answer. The two-party system encourages Americans to think this way, but the reality of public policy is that few, if any, political issues are so simple. The reduction of problems into two sides fosters a mentality of "us" versus "them," complicating bargaining and compromise while decreasing incentives to work together to find workable alternatives.

Likewise, when policy debates turn into two-sided battles of us and them, a common response is to demonize opponents and assume the worst of them. In the midst of a partisan war, we can begin to view our own side as the sole defender of the good and assume our opponents have bad motives. The problem is that most people in politics are trying to do what they believe is right. As we will explore in more detail in chapter 9, political differences are often much less about morality than competing visions of the best way to achieve similar goals. Politicians typically agree on what needs to change; they just disagree on how to do it.

Parties can help voters think through complex issues, but excessive loyalty to party can cloud judgment. The results from many political surveys over the years show that strong partisans often get the facts wrong. An election survey in 1988, for example, asked respondents several questions about the economy. Inflation had declined sharply during Ronald Reagan's years in office, but only 10 percent of the strong Democrats surveyed agreed that inflation had improved. About half of them answered that inflation was worse under Reagan.

The rise of 24-hour cable news, the Internet, and the blogosphere has made it easier than ever for Americans to filter out information they don't want to hear. As a result, many people pay attention only to those news sources that reflect their particular partisan or ideological views. Republicans regularly tune in to Fox News programs, even as many Democrats follow politics on MSNBC. Although it is useful to turn to trusted voices to learn their opinions about political events, listening to a range of viewpoints helps us learn more so we can weigh political alternatives and make more informed judgments.

Countercultural Christians in Partisan Times

As we have seen, political labels can create a useful framework for thinking about public policy. At the same time, however, they are often the source of confusion and divisiveness that can quickly get in the way of our call to love God and neighbor and tempt us to slander others. Looking beyond labels for others and for ourselves is important to our Christian witness, for it reflects a commitment to seeing one another as bearers of God's image. Devotion to party can also distort our views of fellow believers. If you find yourself wondering, "How can they be true Christians and think that way?" partisanship has probably gripped your life too strongly. Far too much of contemporary political debate creates implicit expectations that "good" Christians ally with one political party or the other.

Instead of quickly dismissing people because they do not appear to share our views, we should engage in meaningful conversations that allow for respectful dialogue. Similarly, we should refuse to use labels in a demeaning or insulting manner. Glib remarks such as "conservatives hate poor people" or "those godless Democrats" make a mockery of broad categories of people, showing contempt instead of love for others.

Former Republican Senator John Danforth reflects on some problematic uses of ideological labels in the church, explaining:

> The problem is not that Christians are conservative or liberal, but that some are so confident that their position is God's position that they become dismissive and intolerant toward others and divisive forces in national life. . . . It is no advance to supplant the self-confident religious agenda of the Right with a religious agenda of the Left.[3]

Political commitments, in and of themselves, are not problematic. The problem arises when ideological labels create a barrier between us and those we are called to love and serve in God's name.

In the same way that we should exercise caution when interacting with people who may not share our views, so should we be careful about the role of political labels in our own lives. Ideology and its role in structuring political perspectives can be powerful and enticing. Such frameworks offer quick shortcuts for choosing sides on political issues and for selecting candidates. But the quest for ideological or partisan purity can replace our desire to serve God first in our politics. We should always be on guard to make sure that our Christian commitments, not other ideological commitments, come first.

Now that we have looked briefly at political beliefs, the purpose of political parties, and some of the potential perils of partisanship, let's continue our journey by looking at religion in American government. In particular, the next chapter will discuss some of the myths and realities about the role of religion in the American founding and will look at religion in the Constitution. We'll also consider some different ways to think about the relationship between church and state.

QUESTIONS FOR DISCUSSION

Reflecting

1. What kinds of things do you typically associate with the term "conservative"? With the term "liberal"? How well do these associations match with the descriptions of these ideologies in the chapter?

2. How can political parties make it easier for you to understand and approach politics? How might political parties create confusion and encourage division?

Responding

3. What are some practical steps you can take to make sure that your party loyalty and ideological views do not get in the way of serving God first in politics?

Chapter 6

★ ★ ★

Church, State, and the United States

The church must be reminded that it is not the master or the servant of the state, but rather the conscience of the state.

—MARTIN LUTHER KING JR.

An ad in the *Washington Post* read: "Congratulations, Congressman Pete Stark." Below a large close-up picture of the congressman's face, the ad said, "You're in good company," and displayed smaller photographs of six other men and women. What honor placed Stark in good company with Tufts philosopher Daniel C. Dennett, journalist and author Barbara Ehrenreich, Harvard psychologist Steven Pinker, comedienne and *Saturday Night Live* alumna Julia Sweeney, novelist Kurt Vonnegut, and Harvard biologist Edward O. Wilson? The congressman admitted that he is an atheist.

The American Humanist Association ran the ad congratulating the congressman for his courage. Newspapers across the country carried stories about the thirteen-term legislator's announcement. Why did Stark's description of his religious views capture so much media attention? His remarks made history because he became the highest-ranking politician in the United States to state publicly that he did not believe in God.

Other elected officials likely share Stark's beliefs, but what sets him apart is his public admission of this politically sensitive detail. Americans expect their elected officials to at least appear to be religious. Article VI of the Constitution forbids the government from creating religious tests as qualifications for public office, but unofficially voters can and do impose such criteria. When asked about different traits that might affect their support for presidential candidates, six in ten Americans in a recent survey said they would be less likely to support someone who did not believe in God.

His remarks made history because he became the highest-ranking politician in the United States to state publicly that he did not believe in God.

In much the same way that the Constitution bans official religious tests for office but leaves voters free to apply whatever criteria they choose, some of our expectations about the role of religion in politics follow directly from the Constitution, while some come more from tradition and our personal views. This chapter will consider this interaction, beginning with a brief look at the role of religion in the creation of the United States. After taking a closer look at the Constitution and judicial interpretation of its religion clauses, the chapter concludes by considering some of the ways individuals approach church and state questions.

Religion and the American Founding

Depending on your sources, you are likely familiar with one of two competing tales about the American founding. One story, that of Christian America, describes the United States as an explicitly Christian nation founded on biblical principles by committed believers following God's direction. Using quotes from some of the Founding Fathers to support their arguments, supporters of this view urge faithful Christians to join the fight against secularism, reclaim our godly heritage, and usher in a renewed society based on biblical values.

Opponents of this perspective fire back, contending that the founders had the option to create a Christian government but deliberately chose a secular design. For example, Americans United for Separation of Church and State maintain: "The U.S. Constitution is a wholly secular document. It contains no mention of Christianity or Jesus Christ. . . . Had an officially Christian nation been the goal of the founders, that concept would appear in the Constitution. It does not. Instead, our nation's governing document ensures religious freedom for everyone."[1]

★ ★ ★

In what ways, if any, might it be accurate to describe the United States as a Christian nation?

★ ★ ★

As Christians, what should we make of these competing stories that appear to have such power over Americans? In what ways, if any, might it be accurate to describe the United States as a Christian nation? To answer these and related questions, we will take a brief look at what scholars know about the religious beliefs and practices of the Founding Fathers and consider some of the religious imprints they left on the government they formed.

Faith and the Founding Fathers

The Founding Fathers valued ideals such as personal liberty, equality of opportunity, individual rights, and the need for limited government. Although they shared many common goals, they had sharp disagreements about the best way to design a new government. They found inspiration in various places—personal religious views, political philosophy, and faith in human reason.

Numerous authors have written about the faith of the Founding Fathers with varying levels of academic precision and faithfulness to the historical record. Some writers simply count religious-sounding words in speeches and letters, using word counts as a proxy measure of personal piety. One problem with this technique is that most people living in colonial times were familiar with the Bible and the stories it tells, so biblical and religious references were part of everyday life. In much the same way that people today quote lines from popular songs or television shows, the colonists would likely have quoted the Bible.

In colonial America, as in modern times, more people said they believed in God than genuinely practiced a particular religion. The best (although imperfect) way to look across time to speculate about someone's actual religious beliefs is to look for discussion of religion in private writings, records of church attendance and participation in sacraments, and evidence of other forms of religious activity. The overwhelming consensus of those scholars who research the faith of the Founding Fathers is that few, if any, of them would qualify as evangelicals as we currently use the term. Some of the Founding Fathers appear to have held orthodox Christian beliefs, but most of them (including the most famous) are best described as Deists in some form.

In modern usage, Deism refers to a belief in a distant god who created the universe, set things into motion, and no longer intervenes. At the time of the founding, Deism was a growing movement that typically included five elements: "(1) there is a God; (2) he ought to be worshipped; (3) virtue is the principal element in this worship; (4) humans should repent of their sins; and (5) there is a life after death, where evil will be punished, and the good rewarded." [2] Many Deists agreed with some of the general beliefs of Christianity, but they denied many of the specifics such as the divinity of Christ, the doctrine of the Trinity, and divine revelation.

Like the Deists of their day, most of the founders appear to have shared a general belief in God, the sinfulness of humanity, the need for repentance, and some form of afterlife. A range of religious ideas and values likely had a profound influence on their viewpoints and the government they established, but the historical record finds little evidence that the United States was founded to be a distinctively Christian nation.

Christian Influences on the Structure of American Government

Even though orthodox Christianity was out of favor with most of those who helped craft the Constitution, it is unfair to say they created the United States without regard to religion. The government itself is secular in design, but Christianity and its doctrines exerted a strong influence on its form and structure.

The idea of individuals entering into a covenant for self-government, for example, follows from the idea of covenants with God. Similar to the sinner who receives eternal life through a covenant with God, so could individuals agree to contract with government to provide for the common good. The very first formal document in American political history, the Mayflower Compact of 1620, was a covenant between God and the Puritan settlers that established their government. The two foundational documents for American government, the Declaration of Independence and the Constitution, also reflect aspects of covenantal theology. Although the Constitution never directly mentions God, it creates an agreement between the people and their government that many approach with a sense of sacred obligation.

A READER'S GUIDE TO 18TH
CENTURY RELIGIOUS LANGUAGE

★ ★ ★

A CASUAL READER of documents from the time of the American founding can look at the use of religious words and phrases to help distinguish between Deist and more explicitly Christian thought. Deists, for example, were likely to make only general and Unitarian references to God. In 18th century documents, the following phrases would typically reflect Deism:

- Nature's God
- the Grand Architect
- the Great Author
- the Great Ruler of Events
- the Universal Parent

Trinitarian Christian believers used more precise terminology, speaking of Jesus Christ, His saving grace, and the gospel. In eighteenth-century documents, the following phrases would be common ways of describing more specifically Christian concepts:

- Lord of Hosts
- Saviour
- Almighty God
- all Gracious Providence
- our Divine Redeemer

Another significant Christian principle, the doctrine of human sinfulness, influenced the design of American governing institutions. The founders believed that government was necessary to control sinful people, but they also mistrusted a government that placed power in the hands of sinful people. James Madison outlined this perspective in Federalist #51, an essay written in defense of the Constitution:

> But what is government itself, but the greatest of all reflections on human nature? If men were angels, no government would be necessary. If angels were to govern men, neither external nor internal controls on government would be necessary. In framing a government which is to be administered by men over men, the great difficulty lies in this: you must first enable the government to control the governed; and in the next place oblige it to control itself.[3]

As we saw in chapter 3, the framers of the Constitution created a multilayered system designed to control a government comprised of sinners that, in turn, needed to restrain sinful people.

A third example of Christian influence is the connection between law and morality. Borrowing in large part from the heritage of the Puritans, American political culture places great value on the rule of law. Good citizens follow the law, play by the rules, and live upright lives. For many, the law is an important reflection of public morality; laws help society know right from wrong and hold people accountable for their actions.

As we have seen, the system of government created in the Constitution drew upon both secular and religious ideas. Some of the Founding Fathers appear to have been deeply religious men, while one or two others renounced almost all formal religious beliefs. Although the idea of recapturing the explicitly Christian heritage of the United States is based largely on myth, religion has been and continues to be an important influence on our government.

Religion and the Constitution

The Constitution never mentions God, directly or indirectly. As historian Edwin Gaustad notes, "Unlike most state constitutions of the time, the national document did not mention God even in the vaguest terms of an 'overruling Providence' or 'Grand Architect' of the world or acknowledge the existence of any national creed."[4] The one mention of religion in the original text of the Constitution is the ban on religious tests for office in Article VI. The only other references occur in the First Amendment's religion clauses.

A GODLESS CONSTITUTION?

★ ★ ★

THE DECLARATION OF Independence includes a few generic references to God that reflect the Deism common at that time:

- "the separate and equal station to which the Laws of Nature and of Nature's God entitle them."
- The people are described as "endowed by their Creator with certain unalienable Rights."
- The document ends with the words: "with a firm reliance on the protection of Divine Providence."

In contrast, the United States Constitution does not mention God directly or indirectly.

The First Amendment and Freedom of Religion

The First Amendment reads: "Congress shall make no law respecting an establishment of religion, or prohibiting the free exercise thereof; or abridging the freedom of speech, or of the press; or the right of the people peaceably to assemble, and to petition the Government for a redress of grievances." Taken together, this amendment guarantees several different forms of freedom of expression.

The first sixteen words provide the foundation for religious freedom in the United States. Most discussions shorten the first part, "Congress shall make no law respecting an establishment of religion," calling it the establishment clause. In much the same way, references to the second part, "or prohibiting the free exercise thereof," describe it as the free exercise clause.

The establishment clause is designed to protect against the government backing a particular religion. At the time of the founding, most countries had an official, "established" church supported with tax dollars, and almost all of the American colonies likewise recognized an official state church. The establishment clause charts a new path, forbidding the United States from creating an officially recognized, government-supported church. What else this clause prohibits or permits is a matter of much disagreement. Interpretations range widely from those who say it forbids any government money going to any religious organization to those who claim it allows almost anything short of the government sponsoring a church.

The other religion clause, the free exercise clause, protects freedom of religious belief and practice. The government cannot require anyone to hold any particular religious beliefs, nor can it punish anyone solely for what they profess. Interpretation of this clause gets more complicated, however, when laws or government activities make religious practices difficult or impossible.

The debate over the application of these two clauses has created much controversy, especially in recent decades. Both clauses are vague, and in certain instances the two clauses may conflict. In the words of former Chief Justice Warren Burger, "The Court has struggled to find a neutral course between the two Religion Clauses, both of which are cast in absolute terms, and either of which, if expanded to a logical extreme, would tend to clash with the other."[5]

Consider an example. A public school student may want to freely exercise her religion by reciting a prayer in Jesus' name together with her homeroom class, but this action would inhibit her Muslim classmate's ability to freely exercise his faith. At the same time, the state-funded school would violate the establishment clause if it officially sanctioned the Christian prayer. In practice, Americans are free to worship within certain limits. The government is allowed to interact with religious organizations, but it must respect certain boundaries. Like all political rights that appear absolute in theory, in practice government must place some limits on individual rights to maintain order.

The Supreme Court and the Religion Clauses

The history of legal decisions interpreting the religion clauses is far from consistent. Over time, judicial rulings have tended to alternate between cases that broadly interpret the clauses and cases that read the First Amendment more restrictively.

Establishment Cases and the Lemon Test

Supreme Court decisions sometimes create legal tests that outline criteria for judges to follow in future decisions. The most famous test for establishment cases, the *Lemon* test, gets its name from the case *Lemon v. Kurtzman* (1971), in which the Court agreed to decide three related cases at the same time. Plaintiffs in Pennsylvania and Rhode Island challenged laws that allowed tax dollars to go to religious schools. In Pennsylvania, for example, the state supplemented teachers' salaries and helped purchase books and materials for non-religious courses in parochial schools. Chief Justice Burger wrote for the unanimous court, striking down the laws in both states for violating the establishment clause. Burger's decision set up what we now call the "*Lemon* test," which creates three criteria to determine the constitutionality of laws that affect religious organizations. To pass this test, laws must meet three conditions: (1) they must have a primarily secular purpose, (2) they should neither advance nor inhibit religion, and (3) they must avoid "excessive government entanglement with religion."[6] Applying these criteria, the Court ruled that state funding of non-religious instruction in religious schools was unconstitutional. The Court said that the laws had a secular purpose, but they failed the final two parts of the test because they advanced religion and created excessive entanglement between the government and religious schools.

SEPARATION OF CHURCH AND STATE AND THE CONSTITUTION

★ ★ ★

CONTRARY TO POPULAR belief, neither the Constitution nor the First Amendment includes the phrase "separation of church and state." The metaphor of a "wall of separation" is nothing new. Historians date the phrase back to sixteenth-century Anglican theologian Richard Hooker who used the phrase in his defense of the established church in Great Britain. Writing in the 1640s, Roger Williams used the metaphor to make the opposite argument, defending separation as necessary to protect the church. He described the church as a garden surrounded by the worldly wilderness: "If He will ever please to restore His garden and paradise again, it must of necessity be walled in peculiarly unto Himself from the world; and that all that shall be saved out of the world are to be transplanted out of the wilderness of the world, and added unto His church or garden."[7]

Almost two centuries later, Thomas Jefferson popularized the phrase "wall of separation between church and state" in a short letter written on January 1, 1802. The Baptists, a religious minority in Congregationalist Connecticut, had written a letter congratulating Jefferson on his election. Facing criticism for his unwillingness to declare official days of fasting and thanksgiving, Jefferson decided to use his short reply to the Danbury Baptist Association as an opportunity to defend his views. In a paragraph that begins, "Believing with you that religion is a matter that lies solely between Man & his God, that he owes account to none other for his faith or his worship," Jefferson describes the First Amendment as "building a wall of separation between Church & State." Over a century later, a Supreme Court justice quoted this letter in a landmark decision, ushering Jefferson's metaphor into American political discourse.

Although restrictive, the *Lemon* test leaves some room for formal interactions between government and religious organizations. For example, this test would allow a government program like Medicaid to pay for a patient's surgery at a Catholic hospital. Such a program has a secular purpose—providing health care to the poor. This also passes the test because Catholic hospitals serve everyone regardless of religion and the process for paying the hospital for its services follows the same set of guidelines that would apply to non-religious providers.

The Supreme Court continues to apply the *Lemon* test in some establishment clause cases, but several of the justices currently on the Court think that the test is too restrictive. In recent years, the Court has been more likely to uphold laws that provide indirect aid to religion than those that give funding directly to religious institutions. In the 5-4 decision in *Zelman v. Simmons-Harris* (2002), for example, the Court upheld a program that allowed parents to use tax-supported vouchers to pay for tuition at religious schools.

Free Exercise Cases, the Sherbert Test, and Beyond

The 1963 case of *Sherbert v. Verner* considered the free exercise complaint of Adeil Sherbert, a Seventh Day Adventist who was fired because she refused to work on Saturday, the day her church observed the Sabbath. The state of South Carolina did not accept that she was fired for religious reasons and ruled her ineligible to receive unemployment benefits. In a 7-2 decision, the Supreme Court ruled in favor of Sherbert, arguing that the state violated her free exercise of religion and did not have a compelling interest in denying her unemployment. Justice Brennan's decision created a two-part test for free exercise claims: state laws that interfere with religious practices are only allowed if (1) the state can show it has a "compelling interest" for creating the law (the highest standard of scrutiny to justify the need for a law), and (2) the state cannot achieve its goal any other way without hindering religious observance.

An example of a subsequent case that relied on the *Sherbert* test is *Wisconsin v. Yoder*, the 1972 ruling that Amish parents could opt out of state laws requiring children to attend school until age sixteen. Amish families educated their children through eighth grade; the Court ruled that the added value to the government of assuring students received another year or two of schooling was not compelling enough to justify the strong violation of Amish religious practice.

In the 1990 case *Employment Division v. Smith*, the Court abandoned the *Sherbert* test. Two Oregon drug counselors had used peyote, a hallucinogenic drug, in an Indian religious ceremony. When they failed a drug test, they were fired and denied unemployment benefits. In a 6-3 decision, the Court ruled in favor of Oregon, abandoning the compelling interest test in *Sherbert* and applying less strict standards. They ruled that the law did not specifically target religion and that the state has a reason for prohibiting drug use, so the law was constitutional. *Smith* thus gave states permission to pass and enforce laws that apply generally to all even if the unintended consequences harm some people's freedom to worship.

The outcry was immediate. Conservative and liberal groups demanded action. In response, Congress passed the Religious Freedom Restoration Act of 1993 to reinstate the *Sherbert* test. The new law was short-lived; the Supreme Court overturned it in 1997, arguing that Congress did not have the power to tell the Supreme Court how to interpret the Constitution.

Raising Questions, Seeking Answers: Religion, the State, and the Individual Christian

So far, this chapter has looked at the influence of religion on the founding of America and considered some of the constitutional boundaries for interactions between religion and government. Now it is time to think more about the different ways individual Christians might approach faith and politics.

Every time you check on breaking news stories, head to the polling place, or talk about politics with friends, you are making connections between your faith and your political views. All Christians, regardless of theological or church background, must wrestle with questions about the relationship between religion, the state, and the individual Christian.

Part of the problem is that it is easy to confuse church and state questions with opinions on how personal faith should inform politics. Most Christian believers say that their faith affects how they approach politics as individuals, but they are more likely to disagree in their views about the political role of the church. To add to the confusion, some observers readily associate the phrase "separation of church and state" with strident secularists who want to remove all signs of religion from the public square, forgetting entire traditions of Christian belief that uphold separation out of their religious convictions. Others automatically assume that those whose theological traditions affirm the integration of faith into all realms of life, including government, aim for nothing less than creating a theocracy.

In its formal usage, the phrase "church and state" is generally accepted as shorthand for the connection (or lack of connection) between formal religious organizations and formal governing institutions. In contrast, what I will call "political engagement" questions ask how personal faith convictions should or should not inform citizens' politics. These two categories of questions are interrelated but distinct, and both raise issues that Christians need to consider.

Moving Beyond Simple Categories: A Religion and
Politics Diagram

Far too many discussions of religion and politics begin with assumptions that everyone either supports separation of church and state or wants religion to influence everything. In practice, views on these questions are rarely so sharp and defined. Christians throughout the centuries and across major theological traditions have approached these questions in different ways.

To help you think about the wide range of possible views on

the relationship between religion and politics, consider the diagram, Table 6.1. The chart distinguishes between views on church and state issues and beliefs about religious political engagement, arranging each along the two axes.

The vertical axis of the chart measures views about political engagement. The axis spans from those who are more "engaged with politics," holding the position that political activity is a natural outgrowth of the work of the church, to those who believe the church should be a community "set apart from politics." Should Christian believers participate in politics as a natural outgrowth of their faith, or should they focus primarily on leading people to a deeper relationship with Christ? Is political activity part of sharing and spreading the gospel or is it a distraction from that task? This axis plots your views on these and related questions.

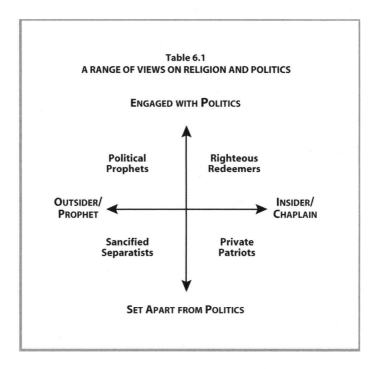

SEPARATING "CHURCH AND STATE" FROM "POLITICAL ENGAGEMENT" QUESTIONS

★ ★ ★

HERE ARE A FEW examples of church and state questions that have been asked over the course of American history:

- Can legislatures begin each day in prayer?
- Should the government print "In God We Trust" on coins?
- Can a city display a manger scene on the lawn in front of City Hall?
- Can public schools begin the day with prayer?

Here are some examples of political engagement questions individuals might ask:

- Should I remove my daughter from sex education courses in her elementary school?
- Should I vote for a candidate who shares my religious views even if I disagree with his stance on many policy issues?
- In what ways should a governmental official's personal religious views affect her conduct in elected office?
- Should I participate in a boycott of a local store under fire for its unfair treatment of workers?

The horizontal axis of the diagram spans from "outsider/prophet" to "insider/chaplain," representing a range of views on the institutional role of the church in relation to government. Is the role of the church more like that of a prophet, intentionally working outside of the system so she can challenge those in power and call them to account when needed? Or is the church more integrated with the state, trying to influence government activity as more of a chaplain who offers religious guidance from within?

When deciding where to place yourself on each axis, consider your theological convictions, views on the role and purpose of government, and personal experiences as you weigh the strengths and weaknesses of each perspective. These tools can help you decide, on balance, where your view best fits.

Your self-placement on each axis will position you in one of four quadrants, what I will describe as Political Prophets, Sanctified Separatists, Righteous Redeemers, or Private Patriots. Those who emphasize God's judgment for collective sinfulness see a strong prophetic role for the church. Political Prophets couple this view with a robust call for political engagement, advocating that the church as an institution should work actively to seek social and political change. In contrast, Sanctified Separatists steer away from a direct role for the church in politics, emphasizing instead the need to separate church from state to maintain the church's purity. From this perspective, the church best shares the gospel by its witness as an alternative community that models Christian love.

Those who emphasize connections between God and nation are generally more supportive of the system and fostering connections between church and state. Righteous Redeemers combine this chaplain perspective with a call for the church to engage actively in politics; some sound the clarion call for renewing a Christian America. Private Patriots also connect their religious practice with their support of the political system, but their disengagement stance leads them to argue for less church involvement in politics. They believe that Christians should apply their faith to politics as part of their private devotion.

Whether you find yourself firmly in one of the four camps or clustered toward the middle, hopefully this diagram helps you understand more about the different ways that Christian believers and different church traditions approach questions about religion and politics. In much the same way that views about the relationship between church and state may not easily fit into discrete categories, it makes sense that these views may also change with time and reflection.[8]

Christian America or American Christians?

As we have seen, religion has influenced American politics from the founding of America to the present day—although not necessarily in all the ways you might expect. The United States is not nor ever has been a Christian nation in the popular use of the term. Biblical concepts and Christian doctrines were among the many ideas that inspired the Founding Fathers as they crafted a new form of government, and aspects of our religious heritage continue to shape the role and function of governmental institutions.

This chapter has also distinguished between two types of questions we need to ask to better characterize our own views on the relationship between our faith and politics. Once we learn to distinguish church and state issues from our perspectives on political engagement, conversation about religion and politics becomes easier and more productive.

The practical value of the distinction between political engagement and church and state questions will likely become clearer to you as we continue our journey together. Now that you know more about what the Constitution does and doesn't say regarding religion and you have a better sense of where to place your own views on the role of religion in politics, you are ready to move to the final section of the book. Each chapter will give you background information and some pointers to help you apply your faith to a different realm of politics. Let's begin by looking at several different models that offer guidance for Christians seeking to connect their faith and politics.

QUESTIONS FOR DISCUSSION

Reflecting

1. What do you think are the most significant Christian influences on American government?

2. What factors do you think help explain the confusion and controversies surrounding judicial interpretation of the First Amendment religion clauses?

3. Where would you place yourself on the religion and politics diagram shown in Table 6.1? Explain why you chose the position that you did.

Responding

4. How can the distinction between "church and state" and "political engagement" questions help us engage in more productive conversations about religion and politics?

PART 3

★ ★ ★

Honoring God in Politics

Chapter 7

★ ★ ★

Connecting Faith and Politics: Different Christian Models

Those who say religion has nothing to do with politics do not know what religion is.

—MAHATMA GANDHI

The tragic events of September 11, 2001, sent shock waves across the United States. Our nation was attacked on its own soil for the first time in over half a century, killing almost 3,000 people. Air travel came to a halt. Millions of Americans waited in fear of what might happen next. What else did the terrorists have planned? Would we ever feel safe again? Who could hate us this much?

As political and military leaders analyzed the scenes of the crime and debated what action to take, everyday Americans responded. Churches and synagogues reported a surge in attendance as people gathered at houses of worship. Flags across the country flew at half staff. Billboards and magnetic signs outside businesses read, "God Bless America." President Bush addressed the nation in a memorial service held at the National Cathedral. Prominent religious leaders gathered at Yankee Stadium for an interfaith prayer service.

As we saw so clearly in the days and weeks immediately following the events of September 11, Americans often turn to faith
in times of crisis and confusion. Some found consolation from their
personal faith, praying and attending worship services that connected them with their God. Others sought solace in public displays
of religion that spoke in general ways about God and country.

God and Country: Civil Religion in America

In times of crisis and in times of relative calm, religion is a
foundation of American political culture. In particular, two kinds
of "religion" provide connections between religion and politics: personal religious beliefs that we might call "private religion" and
those national non-sectarian beliefs, rituals, and creeds social scientists call "civil religion." Private religion provides guidance to
many believers, offering principles that may inform their political
priorities and activities. But the most common and accepted
public displays of religion fall into this second category we call civil
religion. Not a formal written statement of what a nation or government believes nor a government-sanctioned church, civil religion instead refers to a shared understanding of citizenship and
patriotism that uses religious language and symbolism without
direct ties to a particular religion or sect.

Recognizing that civil religion is a significant aspect of our
political culture does not imply that *all* Americans think of the
nation in religious terms, but many or most do, often without
even recognizing that they are making such connections. This
tradition goes back to the founding of America. Sociologist Robert
Bellah traced references to religion in political speech throughout
American history and summarized: "The words and acts of the
Founding Fathers, especially the first few presidents, shaped the
form and tone of the civil religion as it has been maintained ever
since. Though much is selectively derived from Christianity, this
religion is clearly not itself Christianity."[1]

While we find examples of civil religion throughout American history, the fusion of religion and patriotism increases in times of crisis and war. The most recent formal additions to American civil religion came in the 1950s as the Cold War struggle between the United States and the Soviet Union intensified. On June 14, 1954, President Eisenhower signed a bill into law that added the phrase "under God" to the Pledge of Allegiance, reminding Americans of the importance of calling upon God in troubled times: "In this somber setting, this law and its effects today have profound meaning. In this way we are reaffirming the transcendence of religious faith in America's heritage and future; in this way we shall constantly strengthen those spiritual weapons which forever will be our country's most powerful resource in peace and war."[2] Two years later, Congress passed a resolution to replace the original national motto, "E Pluribus Unum," translated "out of many, one" with a new motto, "In God We Trust."

Reach Out and Touch Someone: Politicians and Civil Religion

Generic religious talk is a staple of American political life, as common as campaign signs printed in red, white, and blue. Civil religion is so widely accepted that almost all politicians make broad religious appeals on the campaign trail and when serving in elected office. Candidates routinely sprinkle their public comments with references to God and country, often to thunderous applause. Almost every public event and political speech ends with some version of the phrase "God Bless America." Successful politicians quickly learn that these appeals are great crowd pleasers.

Is religious talk in campaigns anything new? To answer this question, political scientist Roderick Hart analyzed the words used in more than 20,000 speeches, debates, advertisements, and news stories from five decades of campaigns. The results were quite clear: candidates and news coverage in every campaign consistently included references to God, religion, and the Bible. But this religious rhetoric has a particular tone, as if following unwritten rules: "It must be heartfelt but not confessional, frequent but not cloying; pointed but never sectarian. In the United States, at least, political rhetoric must avoid being overly religious, and religious rhetoric overly political."[3] When politicians stray from these expectations, the public notices and reacts negatively—complaining on the one hand if they appear godless or on the other hand if they come off as preachy.

★ ★ ★

Generic religious talk is a staple of American political life, as common as campaign signs printed in red, white, and blue.

★ ★ ★

Although we can see its imprint on expectations of elected officials at all levels of government, civil religion especially shapes public expectations of the president. In speeches and other public appearances, presidents routinely appeal to civil religion and reference divine power. Especially in times of grief or national crisis, the president is expected to calm the nation with comforting religious words and the promise of God's blessing. These expectations are as old as the office. Studies of presidential rhetoric reveal fairly consistent patterns of references to God, biblical stories and verses, and other civil religious language.[4]

PRESIDENTS AND CIVIL RELIGION: AN ENDURING TRADITION

★ ★ ★

CONSIDER A FEW examples of presidential references to civil religion:

And may that Infinite Power which rules the destinies of the universe, lead our councils to what is best, and give them a favorable issue for your peace and prosperity.

THOMAS JEFFERSON, First Inaugural Address;
March 4, 1801

My fellow-citizens, no people on earth have more cause to be thankful than ours, and this is said reverently, in no spirit of boastfulness in our own strength, but with gratitude to the Giver of Good who has blessed us with the conditions which have enabled us to achieve so large a measure of well-being and of happiness.

THEODORE ROOSEVELT, First Inaugural
Address; March 4, 1905

With confidence in our armed forces—with the unbounding determination of our people—we will gain the inevitable triumph—so help us God.

FRANKLIN D. ROOSEVELT, War Message;
December 8, 1941

With a good conscience our only sure reward, with history the final judge of our deeds, let us go forth to lead the land we love, asking His blessing and His help, but knowing that here on earth God's work must truly be our own.

JOHN F. KENNEDY, Inaugural Address,
January 20, 1961

Civil Religion and the Christian Believer

As we have seen, civil religion has a central and enduring place in American political rhetoric and national observances. Such public pronouncements can be beneficial, drawing our attention to God and reminding us of a power greater than ourselves. But civil religion has its limits.

Like so many other good things, devotion to nation can turn into idolatry. Government has a rightful place, and Christians have a role participating in it. But the temptations are great to look to government as a source of renewal, shifting focus away from the true source of renewal—Jesus Christ and His saving grace.

Civil religion may also cloud our judgment. When references to God and country become so commonplace, it is easy to confuse these public displays with genuine religious belief. We may talk about God and politics frequently but think very little about what it means to offer a faithful Christian witness in the public square. To truly honor God in politics, we need to rely less on civil religion and think more about how Christian doctrines and beliefs should influence and shape our approach to politics. Although this is not an easy task, we have resources that can help us connect our faith and politics more directly. Perhaps the most helpful tool is what we call political theology.

Theologies of Politics: Frameworks and Perspectives

Throughout the centuries God has given the gifts of pastors, teachers, and theologians to help the church interpret God's Word and apply its truth to daily life. Through spoken words and written works, ministers of the gospel offer insights into the Bible and the God revealed in its pages. When a pastor delivers a sermon that enriches our understanding of a favorite passage, we appreciate the Bible in a new light and learn more about God. In much the same way, theological traditions create frameworks that help us interpret and clarify biblical truth. Four such traditions—Catholic,

Lutheran, Anabaptist, and Reformed—have developed distinctive political theologies that offer different models for applying the Christian faith to politics.

Each brief overview that follows will describe some of the distinctive emphases of each theological tradition, its perspectives on the role of the church and the state, and its teaching on Christian political participation. To highlight variations in how each tradition applies biblical principles, I summarize these distinctions in Table 7.1 on page 124.

Catholic Political Theology

The history of interaction between the Catholic Church and the state dates back more than a thousand years. For centuries church and state were integrated. Our discussion here, however, will consider contemporary Catholic political theology.

The unity and mission of the Church are central to Catholic teachings. Hallmarks of the faith include particular emphases on the Incarnation, the sacraments, community, and concern for the poor. The model of Christ incarnate as fully God and fully man leads Catholics to place high value on humanity and the natural world, therefore striving for justice and the common good. Celebration of the sacraments connects Christians with Christ and is therefore the center of church life. Catholic teaching also emphasizes God's design for humans to live in community and our resulting responsibility toward one another. A fourth distinctive emphasis, the special concern for the poor, "reflects the tension between the values of poverty and the relief of poverty."[5] The longstanding Catholic commitment to operate schools, hospitals, and charities is an example of the church living out its mission.

Catholic theology views government as part of God's creation; the state has important roles maintaining order, punishing and deterring wrong behavior, and serving justice. The modern Catholic church is a "public church"; that is, the church has a role within

Table 7.1
FOUR TRADITIONS OF POLITICAL THEOLOGY

	Theological Distinctives	View of Government	View of Christian Political Participation
Catholic	Emphasis on Incarnation gives high value to humanity and the natural world Sacraments are at the center of church life God designed humans to live in community; we are responsible for one another Special concern for the poor	Some separation of church and state may be necessary for religious freedom Church can cooperate with government Principle of subsidiarity; government is a necessary but limited agent	Christians should participate Moral obligation to vote, defend their country, and pay taxes Promote peace around the world Notion of a "public church"
Lutheran	Doctrine of justification by faith alone Emphasis on human sinfulness and the Word and sacraments as signs of the gospel "Two kingdoms" principle: life before God and life in society	"Two governments": one for the church, one for the state Government is needed because of sin Government will use force to restrain evil	Christians should participate; the state is a part of God's established order and provides a means for love of neighbor Permits passive resistance to ungodly laws Church should not be directly involved in politics
Anabaptist	Baptism for professing believers; the believers' church Sharp distinctions between church and world Priority of the New Testament, especially teachings of Jesus Non-resistance or pacifism	Government was made necessary after the fall Advocate separation of church and state; the church must be set apart to preserve her purity	Love of neighbor compels Christians not to participate in government Obey secular laws unless they contradict God's commands Emphasis on Jesus' ethic of non-violence
Reformed	Emphasis on the sovereignty of God Emphasis on narrative of creation, fall, and redemption	The state is an agent of common grace Government is fallen but can serve redemptive purposes The primary role of government is to secure justice	Christians should participate in government as agents of transformation Demands obedience to and respect of the state unless an act would contradict God's law Churches can act institutionally to organize political action

political and social life to serve its purpose. Church and state need some separation to guarantee religious freedom, but the church can and should cooperate with government to achieve shared goals.

Following naturally from this perspective on church and state, the church teaches that citizens can and should participate in government. The Catechism outlines three specific moral obligations of all Christian citizens: voting, defending one's country, and paying taxes.[6] But duty to country does not stop at national borders; engagement extends to the entire world community, especially the goal of promoting peace.

Most of the principles that govern the Catholic view of church and state come from Catholic Social Teaching (CST), a tradition officially dating from 1891 that provides principles for preserving faith and living out the gospel when interacting with modern society. Seven key themes comprise the heart of CST: the dignity of all human life; the call to family, community, and participation; rights and responsibilities; preferential care for the poor and vulnerable; the dignity of work; solidarity; and care for God's creation.[7] Balancing these goals means that, in practice, "the political patterns for Catholic advocacy generally defy typical partisan divisions due to their 'progressive' stances on social welfare and labor and 'conservative' positions on abortion and education policy."[8]

Political scientist Clarke Cochran describes four aspects of the church's relationship with politics, culture, and society: cooperating with government to meet certain needs, challenging government policies Catholics believe are wrong, competing with government to provide similar services, and transcending government to further the gospel and follow the Great Commission. Depending on the circumstances and the issues at hand, the church can respond in different ways: "CST incorporates these four modes, recognizing a plurality of applications to particular social and political questions, which gives Catholic social doctrine unique power and flexibility."[9]

The principle of subsidiarity offers guidance to determine what

problems government should address and which issues are better
left to families, churches, or individuals. First introduced in 1931,
subsidiarity is "the idea that government should not replace or
absorb smaller forms of community, but should provide them with
help (*subsidium*) when they are unable or unwilling to contribute
to the common good on their own. The government directs and
coordinates the activities of these smaller units or voluntary associations as needed."[10] Government is an important, necessary, and
limited agent to provide for the common good, but it functions best
in partnership with associations that are close to the people and
best able to meet their particular needs.

Lutheran Political Theology

Modern-day Lutheran denominations trace their roots to the
writings of sixteenth-century Protestant reformer Martin Luther.
Hallmarks of Luther's teachings include the doctrine of justification by faith alone, an emphasis on human sinfulness, and the
priority of the Word and sacraments as signs of the gospel. For the
Christian, good works are not a means to salvation but a natural
response to God's love expressed in love for neighbor: "A Christian lives not in himself but in Christ and his neighbor. Otherwise
he is not a Christian. He lives in Christ through faith, in his neighbor through love. By faith he is caught up beyond himself in God.
By love he descends beneath himself into his neighbor."[11]

At the heart of Luther's teachings are two principles: two
kingdoms and two governments. As historian David Steinmetz
summarizes,

> The two kingdoms refer primarily to the two overlapping spheres
> of Christian existence, the life of the Christian before God and
> the life of the Christian in society. The two governments refer
> to the two ways in which God governs the world. God governs
> the Church through the gospel, a government from which all

forms of coercion are excluded; and he governs the world through law and coercion, a government which cannot achieve its ends through the persuasive preaching of love.[12]

The two kingdoms are distinct but intersecting. The spiritual life of Christians is thus distinguished from their interactions as citizens, but their faith gives meaning and purpose for their service in the kingdom of the world.

★ ★ ★

The state is necessary because of sin.

★ ★ ★

The two governments of Lutheran theology establish very different roles and powers for the church and the state. Christians are subject to both civil and church authority. The church is ordained by God to preach the gospel, teach the Word, and administer the sacraments. Some form of church government is permissible as long as it is not coercive. The state, in contrast, is necessary because of sin. God established government to restrain those who don't know God and fall into wickedness, and to protect citizens and ensure justice for them. Governments can and will use force to restrain evil.

Traditional Lutheran teaching says Christian citizens can participate in government for two central reasons. First, the state is a part of God's established order and therefore a worthy place for Christians to serve. Second, the state provides a means for living out love for neighbor; Christians can and should serve in government because non-Christians need government to ensure justice and punish wickedness. The laws of God are higher than any laws of government, so Christians may choose passive resistance to ungodly laws. Violent resistance is not an option.

The most common contemporary Lutheran application of the two kingdoms doctrine emphasizes different roles for the church and the individual Christian. The church's primary focus is spreading the gospel through preaching the Word and administering the sacraments. The institutional church does not get directly involved in politics but teaches, challenges, and equips its members to love and serve their neighbors. Christians live out their faith as active citizens of both kingdoms: "It is the individual Christian, both as member of the church and citizen of the state, who is duty bound to become the primary 'speaker' of the church's many social concerns. . . . Therefore, individual Christians can, and must, learn to translate the concerns of God's Word into arguments appropriate for civil government."[13] This distinction between the role of the church and its members makes room for individual Christians to disagree on political matters and for Christians to partner in service with those outside the faith.

Anabaptist Political Theology

The term "Anabaptist" emerged in the sixteenth century to describe a wide range of radical reformers who rejected the practice of infant baptism and instead advocated baptism only for those who profess faith in Christ. Their teachings ran counter to those of the state churches of their time, so the early Anabaptists faced great persecution. Many were executed as heretics.

Although this umbrella term includes a wide range of thinkers, some general hallmarks of early Anabaptist thought include sharp distinctions between the church and the world, an emphasis on a church comprised only of professed believers, and a priority on New Testament writings, especially the life and teachings of Jesus. A commitment to pacifism or non-resistance became another distinctive of the movement, one that historian Werner O. Packull describes as "a unique contribution in a violent age." In its earliest expression, non-resistance "means literally accepting power-lessness and abstaining from any use of force or coercion, even self-defence. For Anabaptists, non-resistance was not a calculated survival strategy but a principle for Christian life and conduct; an assumed non-political kingdom ethic revealed by Christ."[14]

The Anabaptist view of the state is similar to the basic structure of the Lutheran two kingdoms doctrine; government is part of the kingdom of the world, the church is part of the kingdom of God. Government is ordained by God, so Christians must obey secular authorities unless their teachings violate God's commands.

A friend of God should not be
in the government but out of it.

Concerned about the corruption within the churches of their day, Anabaptist reformers sought to recover the true church: "The kingdom [of God] was to be made visible in the church, restored to its pristine apostolic purity. True followers of Christ gathered in closely knit, disciplined communities in which the rule and command of Christ prevailed."[15] The church thus stands in contrast to the world as God's witness and community. These beliefs provide the foundation for the Anabaptist call for separation of church and state. To preserve the purity of the church, she must be set apart: "Arguing that the believing Christian community, not government, should govern the church, they rejected over 1,100 years of the union of church and state, demanding instead complete freedom from the state in all matters of religion."[16]

In stark contrast to the Lutheran view that Christians demonstrate love for neighbor through participation in government, most of the early Anabaptist writers "said that a Christian may not participate in government out of love for neighbor. A servant of Christ had no liberty to use coercion and vengeance or to kill because it was contrary to the commandments of Christ."[17] Governments rule by power and force, punishing those who violate the law; Christians, however, must renounce violence and take on love. Christ's command of love for neighbor therefore points the Christian to a different and better path than government: "Insofar as it were possible for a government to act in this way it could well be Christian in its office. Since however the world will not tolerate it, a friend of God should not be in the government but out of it, that is if he desires to keep Christ as Lord and Master."[18]

In contemporary practice, the Anabaptist tradition offers a distinctive model of Christian engagement that emphasizes Jesus' ethic of non-violence and the church's role as the community of Christ. Jesus makes radical and countercultural demands, and Christians must seek to follow them. In keeping with their pacifist heritage, modern Anabaptists usually hold one of two views on government and the use of force. Some actively seek to influence government in ways consistent with Jesus' ethic of non-violence. Others argue that violence is always outside God's will. Because this tradition promotes faithfulness to Christ's teaching through work as an active community of believers, Anabaptists are most likely to seek change through work and advocacy outside of government.

Reformed Political Theology

The Reformed tradition developed from the writings and teachings of noted sixteenth-century Protestants such as John Calvin, John Knox, and Ulrich Zwingli. Hallmarks of this tradition include an emphasis on the sovereignty of God and use of the narrative of creation, fall, and redemption as a framework for understanding God's interaction with humanity. Creation refers both to God's original creative acts and also to the mandate for humans to "fill the earth and subdue it." As such, institutions like the family and the state were designed and established by God as part of the perfect created order.

Because of the fall, sin affects humans in all aspects of their lives. God's grace extends to the fallen world in two ways. The first type, particular grace, refers to the saving grace God extends to those whom He calls. A second form of grace, common grace, "is experienced in the ordering of nature, the restraint of evil and the ability of unbelievers to reason and perform acts of civil good. The doctrine of common grace holds that God bestows on humanity a grace that, while not 'saving,' enables unbelievers to develop many virtues and express many truths."[19] The state is one agent of this common grace.

The final piece of the gospel narrative, redemption, applies to all of creation. Just as individuals can receive personal redemption from their sins, so can institutions "become agents of redemption (not in terms of salvation but of transformation) in the society and world at large, fulfilling their original purpose by bringing about a right ordering of human interrelationships."[20] Although corrupted by the fall, government can thus serve a redemptive purpose. Complete redemption is impossible until Christ returns, but Christians must join in the work of renewal while they await the full restoration available only in Christ.

John Calvin wrote that God ordained government and holds its leaders accountable to Him, so Christians must obey and respect the state. Contempt for government is not an option, for "to despise human government is to despise the providence which set that government in place. Rules must be obeyed, not on the grounds of human necessity, but on the grounds of obedience to God."[21] Furthermore, Christians can and should participate in government, as in all spheres of life, seeking to transform fallen institutions and structures.

One contemporary application of Reformed teaching is the concept of "principled pluralism," derived in large part from the work of Dutch Reformed theologian and former Prime Minister of the Netherlands, Abraham Kuyper. Building from Kuyper's discussion of sphere sovereignty, society includes different institutions or spheres ordained by God, serving different roles, and working independently from one another. The state is one of these spheres that ensures justice in and between the different institutions of society. Constitutional law and representative government constrain the state's power. In contrast to the Lutheran and Anabaptist restrictions of the church's mission to evangelism, discipleship, and mercy, the Reformed tradition makes room for churches to advocate for particular policies or organize political action.

Principled pluralism begins with recognition of the wide range of religious worldviews. It is not the role of the state to endorse a particular religion; instead, government should guarantee freedom of religion. The state is one of many structures in society designed by God, so its powers should be limited. The primary role of government is to secure justice—in the negative sense of protecting its citizens from harm, and in the positive sense of promoting the common good. Governments cannot and should not try to impose morality, for "the task of government is not to compel everything that is right or moral, nor to punish everything that is wrong or immoral, but to enforce that particular part of morality we call justice. . . . Because morality is a matter of the heart, no one can be forced to be moral."[22] Christians must discern what tasks are best suited for what spheres of influence, not expecting too much or too little from government.

Asking Questions, Seeking Answers: Faithful Politics

The brief discussions above are intended as introductions, not definitive treatments, of these four theologies of politics. All of these frameworks demand that believers move beyond civil religion to think more deeply about how specific religious doctrine and application can help us honor God in politics. Each tradition brings new ideas to the table to help shape our thinking about the role of the church, the purpose of the state, and the place for Christian participation in politics and government.

As we have seen, Christians across time have answered these questions differently and offer insights for believers struggling with how to approach these complex issues. Some of you have seen a version of your own faith tradition reflected here; others will find you may not fit comfortably in any of the four traditions sketched in this chapter. Even so, to develop our own understanding of how Christianity should inform politics, we need to wrestle with these central questions about the role and function of government, the relationship between church and state, and the proper place (if any) for Christians to engage in politics and government.

Now that you understand more about some of the most influential theologies of politics, you can see how followers of Christ can in good faith reach varied conclusions about political questions. Christians from the various theological traditions will have different assumptions about what government can and should do, just as they may find very different ways to address political dilemmas. As we seek to apply our faith to politics, we need to be aware of our own theological and ideological assumptions and be willing to engage others about theirs.

This chapter has introduced various theological perspectives on the personal and institutional role of religion in government to help you better characterize your own views. The next two chapters will explore some of the complexities of public policy to better prepare you to advocate for issues that concern you. Let's begin by looking at some of the reasons it can be so difficult to talk honestly and charitably about political issues and consider some practical ways we can be faithful Christian witnesses in the public square.

QUESTIONS FOR DISCUSSION

Reflecting

1. What are some of the potential benefits of civil religion? What are some of the limits of civil religion?

2. Which aspects of each of the traditions of political theology described in this chapter appeal to you? Why? Which aspects raise questions in your mind?

Responding

3. The author suggests that "as we seek to apply our faith to politics, we need to be aware of our theological and ideological assumptions and be willing to engage others about theirs." What are your theological and ideological assumptions? What are some ways you can encourage constructive engagement with others who hold different views?

Chapter 8

★ ★ ★

From Diatribe to Dialogue: How to Disagree about Politics Peacefully

The men the American people admire most extravagantly are the most daring liars; the men they detest most violently are those who try to tell the truth.

—H. L. MENCKEN

Speech is a mirror of the soul; as a man speaks, so he is.

—PUBLILIUS SYRUS

Concerned about the increasingly harsh tone of public discourse, Republican businessman and political adviser Mark DeMoss launched the Civility Project in January 2009. DeMoss enlisted Democratic lobbyist and former Clinton aide, Lanny Davis, to help him. Together the two friends wrote to all 100 United States senators, all 435 members of the House of Representatives, and all 50 state governors asking them each to sign a pledge: "I will be civil in my public discourse and behavior. I will be respectful of others whether or not I agree with them. I will stand against incivility when I see it." How many of the 585 recipients agreed? Only three.

Two years later, DeMoss wrote to the three legislators who had signed the pledge, Independent Senator Joseph Lieberman and

Republican Representatives Frank Wolf and Sue Myrick, informing them of his decision to close the Civility Project. "You three were alone in pledging to be civil," DeMoss wrote. "I must admit to scratching my head as to why only three Members of Congress, and no governors, would agree to what I believe is a rather low bar."[1]

Although thousands of private citizens showed their support by signing the pledge, others attacked the work of the project. In an interview with a journalist, DeMoss described his surprise and dismay at the hostile response he received from some of his fellow conservatives: He said that some of the emails contained "unbelievable language about communists, and some words I wouldn't use in this phone call. This political divide has become so sharp that everything is black and white, and too many conservatives can see no redeeming value in any liberal or Democrat."

Why were so few of the nation's leaders willing to take such a simple and seemingly uncontroversial public stand? Why did so many Web users respond to a call for civility and respect with vulgarity and vicious attacks? What might these events reveal about the tone of today's political dialogue?

"You three were alone in pledging to be civil,"
DeMoss wrote. "I must admit to scratching my
head as to why only three Members of Congress,
and no governors, would agree to what
I believe is a rather low bar."

★ ★ ★

Today's hyper-partisan and mean-spirited political climate makes it very difficult to engage in civil and meaningful conversations about politics. When simple differences in perspective quickly turn into heated battles, temptations increase to lash out at opponents and mischaracterize their motives. If we want to honor God in politics, however, we must avoid such hateful talk. James 4:11 commands us to "not speak evil against one another," an exhortation that should extend beyond how we treat other believers. We must engage our political opponents respectfully, welcome the opportunity to learn from other perspectives, and find ways to disagree charitably as a natural part of the political process.

Let's begin by looking at some of the ways in which confusion over the ends and means of public policy can get in the way of honest and open public debate. In particular, we will consider two broad categories of political issues, so-called easy issues and hard issues, and discuss the specific challenges that each set of policies creates for meaningful political dialogue.

Talking about Public Policy: The Role of Ends and Means

Have you ever wondered why politicians always seem to be fighting with each other? Does it seem like the government takes too long to address a problem or cannot fix it? If you have pondered these or similar questions, you are not alone. One of the reasons policy debates can seem so frustrating is that much of the work of government is trying to solve problems that have no easy solutions. If a problem can be addressed easily, government quickly acts and solves it. Everything else—the complex, seemingly hopeless issues—is left for public debate.

"Easy" and "Hard" Issues

One way that political scientists sometimes divide political issues is to think of them in two categories: "easy" issues or "hard" issues. When asked if government should allow gay marriage, for example, most people can answer quite quickly either yes or no. This is what we call an "easy" issue. On the other hand, if you ask someone whether the government should try to stop terrorism, almost everyone (except perhaps terrorists and their sponsors) would immediately say yes. But when you ask the necessary follow-up question—what should we do?—the early consensus quickly disintegrates. Terrorism is a perfect example of a "hard" issue. Almost everyone agrees on the end goal but disagrees on the means of achieving it. Policy debates over terrorism are not about if we should stop terrorism but how we can stop it most effectively.

We use the term "easy" issues—a misnomer for sure—for those issues on which people quickly and instinctively choose a side. Typically, easy issues are presented as if they have only two sides: someone is either for something or against it; there is a right side and a wrong one with little room for middle ground. The categories appear simple because the focus is sharply and intently on the end goal. Most so-called moral issues fall into this category; people typically view abortion, gay marriage, and the sale of narcotics as easy issues.

Unlike those issues that appear to be black and white, "hard" issues are by definition complex. The debate over hard issues is rarely about end results and almost always about means. The center of controversy on these subjects is not the desired policy goal—almost everyone agrees about what needs to be done. Disagreements emerge and multiply as people debate the best way to accomplish a goal and weigh the relative importance of this problem compared with all the other matters government might address. Classic examples of hard issues include ending poverty, protecting national security, and maintaining a healthy economy. Voters almost always agree with such goals; the problem is figuring out the best way to achieve them and when it makes sense for government to try.

When We Disagree on Ends and Fail to Talk about Means

Because the discussion on easy issues typically focuses on ends, not means, activists often frame the debate in absolutist terms, directly or indirectly telling voters that compromise is not only impossible but may even be immoral. Political debates over moral issues often use the language of black and white, us versus them, right and wrong. Such stark contrast offers little space for shades of gray.

★ ★ ★

Activists often have strong incentives
not to seek solutions.

★ ★ ★

And herein lies the problem. As we saw in chapter 2, bargaining and compromise are essential to the political process. To an outside observer, an easy issue appears to have two distinct sides, but in reality government likely has multiple options for addressing all or parts of the issue. As soon as people take sides and stake claims as either for or against a particular end goal, the door closes on possibilities for cooperating to find solutions. Some issues really have two distinct sides that require making a choice. But the subject matter of many so-called easy issues is multifaceted and complex. On such issues, it often makes sense to look to government to address part of the larger problem.

Why don't we look more often for areas of potential political agreement? One reason is that activists often have strong incentives *not* to seek solutions. Ironically, divisive rhetoric that keeps the debate raging also fills their bank accounts. Potential donors are much more likely to contribute to a cause if the stakes are high and the situation appears dire.

When We Agree on Ends and Disagree on Means

What about the other category of issues, those so-called hard issues? How do politicians, activists, and voters approach these kinds of policy problems? Ironically, it is usually easier to debate "hard" issues and find room for political compromise. When people recognize instinctively that an issue is complex, they are more open to considering various policy alternatives. At the same time, they are also more willing to accept partial solutions as productive and valuable steps toward solving larger problems. Debate over hard issues can grow intense and polarizing, but most elected officials and activists enter the discussion fully aware that bargaining will be necessary.

Honest differences in opinion about what
policy is best can quickly turn into accusations,
distortions, and lies.

★ ★ ★

Although successful public policy is almost always the result of compromise, the public rhetoric on hard issues often ignores this political reality. In the same way that divisive language can rally the troops on easy issues, politicians often find that they can capture voter attention with polarizing remarks that demean their opponents' positions and question their motives. Even though the opposing sides agree on the end goal of hard issues, many of the political arguments tossed back and forth distort this truth and magnify disagreements. Honest differences in opinion about what policy is best can quickly turn into accusations, distortions, and lies.

LEGISLATING ACROSS
THE EASY ISSUES DIVIDE

★ ★ ★

POLITICIANS WHO HOLD moderate positions on easy issues often face criticism from activists who expect them to always take their side. Consider Rep. Leonard Lance, a moderate Republican from New Jersey. Although he describes himself as pro-choice on the abortion issue, he joined forces with many pro-life legislators when he voted against federal funding for Planned Parenthood and opposed a bill requiring pharmacists to fill prescriptions for birth-control pills. Those votes led some abortion activists to publicly question his pro-choice credentials. Jackie Cornell from Planned Parenthood Action Fund of New Jersey, for example, reacted harshly to Lance's votes: "I don't know how someone can call themselves pro-choice but then join with the most extreme anti-choice zealots in opposing common sense measures like protecting access to birth control at pharmacies or ensuring women have access to family planning services."[2]

TALKING ABOUT HARD ISSUES

★ ★ ★

SOME POLITICAL LEADERS respond to heated debates with careful, reasoned arguments that can open a path for meaningful dialogue. Consider an editorial published on Politico.com in the midst of a looming debt crisis in the summer of 2011. When Democrats and Republicans appeared at an impasse over how to deal with the nation's growing debt, former U.S. comptroller general David Walker and Robert Bixby of the Concord Coalition called for meaningful, bipartisan dialogue to address the nation's fiscal problems, explaining: "Such sweeping reforms are likely to be politically difficult, so the American people's active involvement is essential. We need a real national dialogue about the massive fiscal challenge, related risks, possible options and the inescapable trade-offs among those options." Exhorting leaders in both parties to speak with civility and seek needed compromise, they concluded: "Despite the heated rhetoric, neither side is blameless for our current predicament—and neither has a monopoly on American values."[3]

Although it is indeed possible to find and claim common ground while also advocating different approaches to solving a problem, such civility is uncommon in today's politically charged climate. In media appearances, press releases, and constituent communications, activists and politicians can choose how they frame their support of and opposition to policy proposals.

Toward Faithful Political Engagement

In the midst of a raging political debate, it is difficult to step back from the battle lines and make careful and reasoned assessments of what a proposed policy is likely to achieve. But if we want our faith to inform our political actions and offer a positive Christian witness, such a measured approach is not only wise—it is essential. Consider three practical ways we can demonstrate our faith in the political arena.

Step One: Admit the Complexity of Political Issues

The first step toward more faithful political engagement begins with awareness of the particular tensions created in policy debates over so-called easy and hard issues. We must recognize that many issues that seem simple at first glance look much more complex once you dig deeper; compromise may be not only possible but wise or even necessary. Likewise, we may be able to tackle those hard issues and large-scale problems that seem so overwhelming if we accept that we cannot fix everything at once.

Many policymakers and citizens talk and act as if they can solve most public policy problems in one easy step. A strong declarative sound bite—"We will win this battle overnight!"—captures more attention and praise than an outline of a multistep, and likely more accurate, path in the right direction. Who wants to hear an elected official admit that a problem is so challenging that perhaps the best government can do is address a few pieces of it over time? American voters are much more likely to respond to optimism than pragmatism, so politicians love to promise quick fixes. In reality, few can deliver them. As long as voters respond so enthusiastically to pledges of easy solutions, few candidates will have the courage to speak frankly about the dilemmas government needs to confront.

One way we can serve those in public office is accepting when they have to make hard choices. When we expect and demand instant results from a slow and complex political system, we make it much harder for government officials to do their very demanding jobs. We should call our leaders to account when they take positions we disapprove of, but we should also allow them the opportunity to explain the choices they made and give them a fair hearing.

American voters are much more likely to respond to optimism than pragmatism, so politicians love to promise quick fixes.

We should also be slow to react to attempts to scare us. Instead of immediately jumping to conclusions when someone sends an alarming email or letter, investigate the claims and do a little research. Their claims may indeed be valid, but often you may discover that they used exaggeration to capture your attention. If a story seems too outlandish to be true, it probably is. If advocates claim a policy proposal will fix a major problem overnight, their pronouncements are likely overblown. The sidebar "Fact Checking at Your Fingertips," lists some websites that can help you test the truth of political claims before you react.

Step Two: Play Fair in the War of Words

An additional and crucial step for Christians in politics is to stand firm against mean-spirited, false, and misleading political talk. So much contemporary political debate shows few signs of nuance and creates a harmful Christian witness. We should not engage in vicious attacks, nor should we support others who do so. Instead, we should encourage honest and open dialogue, raising concerns and criticisms when needed and keeping politicians accountable for their actions.

Before speaking about political opponents or characterizing their positions, apply the simple test of the golden rule. Would you want someone speaking of you and your policy positions in the same way that you speak of them? It may seem impractical to use such criteria, but practicality is not the end goal for the Christian. In political dialogue as in all other interactions, we must first and foremost honor God. It is possible to model an alternative path, avoiding polarizing and uncharitable characterizations of those who hold different views.

Before speaking about political opponents
or characterizing their positions, apply
the simple test of the golden rule.

Instead of playing by the typical rules of the game, Christians can "play fair," choosing rhetoric that shows respect for their opponents while advocating different political means to achieve their goals. In the same way, policymakers can encourage cooperation and model a different form of political engagement, explaining what policy they believe offers the best means for achieving a goal without demeaning those who disagree.

FACT CHECKING AT YOUR FINGERTIPS

★ ★ ★

DO YOU FEEL overwhelmed by all the claims politicians make? Do you wonder which of those Internet rumors you should believe? Did the latest political message in your email in-box raise more questions than it answered? If you have ever struggled with questions like these, help is only a few mouse-clicks away. Here are a few trustworthy websites that can help you sort through the many claims to separate truth from fiction.

Factcheck.org tests the specific claims made in political advertisements, debates, speeches, fundraising letters, and widely circulated emails, reporting what they find to be true, partly true, false, misleading, or exaggerated. The site's "Ask FactCheck" feature gives visitors the chance to check the accuracy of political rumors they may hear. Funded primarily by the Annenberg Foundation and staffed by journalists, Factcheck lives up to its claim of holding politicians accountable. The organization appears to be equally zealous in verifying statements from Democrats and Republicans alike.

The St. Petersburg Times runs the Pulitzer Prize–winning **Politifact.com**, a website that tests the accuracy of political claims from national politicians and in a handful of states. They measure claims on the "Truth-O-Meter" that ranges from true to "pants on fire," the moniker attached to those claims that are not merely false but deemed "ridiculous." Quick links offer details of the extensive research used to test each claim. Politifact keeps an

ongoing tally of presidential and congressional campaign promises, reporting the results on the
"Obameter" and the "GOP Pledge-O-Meter." Easy to
navigate tabs connect visitors to recent fact checks
of claims from widely circulated emails, popular
conservative and liberal pundits, and political candidates.

Although it is a more general site testing claims
on a range of subjects, **Snopes.com** is an excellent
resource for checking the truth of political rumors
that circulate widely on the Internet. Professional
researchers Barbara and David Mikkelson run the
website. Users can enter terms into a searchable
database; each entry includes the particular claim
being tested, its status as true or false, examples
of emails or posts making the claim, details that
help explain the origins of the claim, and the date
the entry was last updated.

Step Three: Advocate for "Hard Issues"

Christians also need courage to enter the much more complex
political waters of the "hard" issues. Many Christians focus almost
all of their attention on the so-called easy issues that raise cultural
concerns. Issues of personal morality are important and need to
be a part of public debate; some people are called in particular to
raise awareness of these issues and challenge the church to
respond. But such issues represent a tiny fraction of the policies
and proposals facing elected officials each year. If Christians focus
almost all of their political attention on these issues, they lose the
opportunity to contribute to the public debate on the wide range
of policies on the political agenda.

Political dialogue about hard issues is often complex, and disagreement is common within the church. It can be uncomfortable when others do not share our policy views, especially when we disagree with other Christians. But concern about disagreement with one another should not keep us from seeking ways to address the wide range of problems affecting us and our world.

We must be careful to avoid the trap of assuming God is on our side simply because our human interpretation suggests it.

★ ★ ★

Honoring God in Our Political Talk

As we have seen, elected officials and activists often share similar policy goals but disagree about the best ways to achieve them. Much of current political debate is harsh and deceitful. As followers of Christ, we can provide a powerful countercultural witness by modeling our faith as we engage with politics.

Many Christians enter public debate assuming that they know God's truth on a particular issue. The Bible contains God's truth, and we can seek to know that truth. But we must interpret the Bible in order to understand it, and human interpretations can and do fail. Knowing these limitations, we must be careful to avoid the trap of assuming God is on our side simply because our human interpretation suggests it.

When someone begins a conversation with the assumption that the truth is clear and his or her side is right, meaningful dialogue and mutual respect can seem almost impossible. But if we enter political debates with the assumption that our opponents are sincere and acting in good conscience even if we think they are wrong, this opens a path for extending charity and respect. In 2 Peter 1:5–8, the apostle encourages his fellow believers to

make every effort to add to your faith goodness; and to good-ness, knowledge; and to knowledge, self-control; and to self-control, perseverance; and to perseverance, godliness; and to godliness, mutual affection; and to mutual affection, love. For if you possess these qualities in increasing measure, they will keep you from being ineffective and unproductive in your knowl-edge of our Lord Jesus Christ.

Imagine how our politics could be transformed if we sought these qualities in all our interactions!

In the next chapter, we will look more carefully at some of the reasons why Christians disagree about how to achieve their polit-ical goals. After giving you some tools for applying biblical truth to public policy, we will walk through a real-life example, consid-ering different approaches Christians might advocate and sug-gesting ways to engage in respectful and constructive debate.

QUESTIONS FOR DISCUSSION

Reflecting

1. Thinking about current events in the news right now, which ones would you classify as "easy issues" and which as "hard issues"? Explain your reasoning.

2. In what ways are the terms "easy issues" and "hard issues" useful and descriptive? What are some of the potential problems with these phrases?

Responding

3. Offer a few examples of ways to discuss and debate policy differences that "play fair" and demonstrate love for neighbor.

Chapter 9

★ ★ ★

Can Christians Honestly Disagree? Applying Faith to Policy Problems

Even if you believe there's only one way to get to heaven, you can still believe there is probably more than one way to balance the budget.

—RALPH REED

The Saturday before the 2010 federal elections, an estimated 215,000 people gathered on the national mall in Washington, D.C. More than 2 million viewers watched the live television broadcast, and another 570,000 streamed the video on their computers. Celebrity guests included pop music stars, sports legends, actors, and a robot (R2-D2 of Star Wars fame). Major domestic and international news outlets covered the events.

What cause drew so many people to the nation's capital? Who was able to attract such a following? Jon Stewart and Stephen Colbert, comedians and hosts of two popular satiric news shows on Comedy Central, staged two coordinated rallies. On one end of the mall, Stewart hosted the "Rally to Restore Sanity" that called for reasonable political discourse. On the other end, Colbert mocked political fear-mongering at his "March to Keep Fear Alive." Participants in the crowd held up hand-lettered signs with slogans such as "Stark raving reasonable," "Civil is sexy," "I disagree with you, but I'm pretty sure you're not Hitler," and "Things are pretty okay."[1]

At the end of the day, Stewart closed the events with more serious remarks explaining his purpose in organizing the rally. He criticized cable news outlets and pundits for promoting extreme rhetoric and complicating political problem solving. Contending that most Americans want a more reasonable tone and are willing to compromise when needed, he noted: "Where we live our values and principles form the foundations that sustain us while we get things done, not the barriers that prevent us from getting things done. Most Americans don't live their lives solely as Democrats, Republicans, liberals or conservatives."[2]

Cable news pundits are not the only ones who need a sanity check. Many Christian activists and politicians mischaracterize their opponents' positions and hurl harsh accusations back and forth as if they were at war. Often by implication (and occasionally in direct attacks), Christians accuse their political opponents of godlessness.

Combative rhetoric captures headlines and garners attention. But it oversimplifies complex political issues and distorts honest differences. In reality, people often disagree on public policy matters for legitimate reasons. That may be true even for Christians: we can in good faith hold to biblical truth yet reach different conclusions about how to apply God's truth to politics.

As we saw in the last chapter, policy problems that we often describe as "hard issues" test the limits of political systems. Because most observers share end goals but disagree on the best means to achieve them, disagreements are inevitable. This chapter explores this reality by looking at the political debate over a classic hard issue, poverty. After a brief discussion of ways to search Scripture to help us think about public political issues, we'll look at a few examples of what the Bible says about poverty and consider some of the possible ways Christians might approach this problem. The chapter concludes with some thoughts about how to interact charitably with others even when we disagree.

Approaching the Bible in Context

The Scriptures are an invaluable resource for Christians seeking to apply their faith to their daily lives. Although the Bible reveals God's truth, our human interpretations of it can and do fall short. Moreover, the Bible focuses on presenting the story of God's love for us in Christ rather than describing specific political policies. Scripture addresses all we need for daily life by pointing us to the One in whom all things hold together (Colossians 1:17). How can Christians avoid misusing Scripture? Equally important, how can we faithfully apply biblical truth to political questions?

Many tools can help you read the
Bible theologically and apply its truth
to political questions.

A first step is avoiding over-simplistic proof texts. In its negative connotation, proof-texting refers to the practice of misusing single Bible verses or fragments of them, alone or strung together with others, to claim biblical justification for an idea or practice. Christians should be cautious not to twist the meaning of a Bible verse for personal ends. At the same time, theologian Daniel Treier reminds us: "For all its deserved derision, however, some concept of 'proof text' seems essential to Christian theology. . . . If God says what the Bible says, we logically pursue the development and

defense of theological claims on such a basis."[3] The key is not
taking individual verses out of context but instead fitting any verse
or (ideally) longer passages into the larger biblical pattern.

Many tools can help you read the Bible theologically and apply
its truth to political questions. Biblical scholars and theologians
have written an array of resources, study Bibles, and reference guides
that offer much guidance. Another way to avoid misleading proof-
texting is to approach the Bible with attention to literary style and
use of language. Often without thinking about it, we read the Bible
with an eye for literary style. When Jesus tells His disciples, "I am
the vine; you are the branches" (John 15:5), for example, most readers immediately recognize the use of metaphor. Jesus is not saying
that He is an actual grapevine; He uses the image of the vine and
branches as a concrete example to help the disciples understand their
true relationship with Him. In the same way that readers can recognize literary devices like metaphor, so can we distinguish between
history, law, poetry, prophecy, and pastoral teaching, recognizing the
particular purpose of each genre.

Searching for Biblical Guidance

Although there are many ways to read the Bible theologically,
one helpful method is to begin with a paragraph-length passage
and move outward. If you want to understand what the Bible
teaches about a particular subject, start first by finding a few relevant passages and reading them in their context. Second, follow
the verses and see where they lead. Does the passage quote other
Scripture? For further insight, look for additional Old and New
Testament passages that also relate to the theme. The comparison
of related sections from different books of the Bible reveals important patterns and consistent emphases.

Consider a simple example. In John 12:8, Jesus tells His disciples: "You will always have the poor among you, but you will not
always have me." What does this verse tell us about Jesus' view of

the poor? Should we ignore the poor and focus on serving Jesus? By itself, the verse seems rather puzzling. But once the verse is placed in its larger context, its meaning becomes clearer. The narrative of John 12 begins in Bethany a week before the crucifixion. After hosting a banquet honoring Jesus, Mary anoints Jesus' feet with expensive perfume. Verses 5 and 6 record Judas Iscariot's questioning response: " 'Why wasn't this perfume sold and the money given to the poor? It was worth a year's wages.' He did not say this because he cared about the poor but because he was a thief; as keeper of the money bag, he used to help himself to what was put into it." In these verses, John reveals Judas's corrupt motivations for asking the question in the first place, information that sheds new light on Jesus' response. In addition, the narrative continues as Jesus chastises Judas and affirms Mary: " 'Leave her alone,' Jesus replied. 'It was intended that she should save this perfume for the day of my burial. You will always have the poor among you, but you will not always have me.' " By considering John 12:8 in the context in which it appears, we find the verse already making more sense.

If we follow the next step, we learn even more. A listing of internal cross-references shows that Jesus quoted from Deuteronomy 15:11 in His reply to Judas. Part of a longer section of laws concerning cancellation of debts and caring for the poor, the particular verse reads: "There will always be poor people in the land. Therefore I command you to be openhanded toward your brothers and toward the poor and needy in your land." Jesus references the Mosaic law in His reply to Judas, pointing him (and us) to God's command of generosity to the poor.

As this simple example demonstrates, a single Bible verse in isolation may at times confuse more than it clarifies. What could be read at first glance as minimizing the need to care for the poor reveals quite the opposite when viewed in context. Reading the passage surrounding a verse and finding cross-referenced Scriptures are two tools that can improve our understanding of Scripture. In much the same way, reading and comparing multiple texts on similar subjects adds richness and meaning.

Addressing Poverty in the United States: A Case Study

With some tools for biblical interpretation in mind, let's apply these steps to public policy. How do we determine the best way for Christians to approach a political issue? What steps should we follow? As with any other issue, the first step in seeking God's direction is looking to the Bible to see what, if anything, it says about it. If the Bible does not speak directly about a particular issue, look for biblical insights on related principles that may help guide your decision making.

The Biblical Mandate to Serve the Poor

Scriptures describe God's active concern for defending the fatherless and widows, hearing the cries of the poor, rescuing them, and giving them refuge. From Genesis through Revelation, the Bible includes more than 2,000 verses that talk about the poor and needy. A comprehensive analysis of so many texts would require books in and of themselves, so for the purpose of this short case study, we'll look at just a few biblical themes concerning the poor.[4]

The Bible describes several reasons for poverty. In some verses in Proverbs and some of Jesus' parables, the Bible says laziness can lead to poverty, yet many others blame the wealthy who get rich by exploiting the poor. The travails of the Israelites reveal how God sometimes allows poverty as judgment for sin. But many other biblical references reveal systemic and institutional causes of poverty.

Although the causes of poverty are complex, the response God commands is clear. Reflected in the history of the Israelites, the wisdom books, the words of the prophets, and the New Testament, the Bible clearly condemns oppression. It is evil to exploit the poor and deprive them of justice. Consider part of a passage from the prophecy of Amos:

> *You trample on the poor*
> *and force him to give you grain.*
> *Therefore, though you have built stone mansions,*
> *you will not live in them;*
> *though you have planted lush vineyards,*
> *you will not drink their wine.*
> *For I know how many are your offenses*
> *and how great your sins.*
> *You oppress the righteous and take bribes*
> *and you deprive the poor of justice in the courts.* (Amos 5:11–12)

This passage and many others like it call attention to structural sins and political actions that deliberately prey upon the poor. To gain at the expense of the poor is sin.

It is not just sinful to exploit the poor; the Bible also makes it clear that God commands us to care for them and meet their needs. In the gospel of Matthew, Jesus warns His disciples about the final judgment, making sharp distinctions between the righteous and the unrighteous. In the famous passage we often call "the sheep and the goats," Jesus divides the two by their response to the hungry, strangers, prisoners, and others in need, separating those who cared for the needy from those who ignored them. The story ends with sobering words directed at those who failed to respond: "[The King] will reply, 'I tell you the truth, whatever you did not do for one of the least of these, you did not do for me. Then they will go away to eternal punishment, but the righteous to eternal life'" (Matthew 25:45–46). Passages throughout the Old and New Testaments remind us to care for the most vulnerable in society as part of our love for God and neighbor.

From Consensus to Conflict

As we have seen, biblical teaching about poverty is quite clear. God cares for the poor and commands His children to care for them as well. The Bible condemns people and institutions that exploit others for personal gain. Concern for the poor and the oppressed is one of the marks of true discipleship. Given this teaching, it seems natural that Christians will embrace poverty reduction as a biblical goal.

Agreeing that Christians should care about the problem, however, is the easy step. The remaining questions are far more complicated: What means are best to achieve the end goal? For this example, what is the best way to address the problem of poverty in the United States? What should Christians do to live out the biblical mandate? As is the case with any "hard issue," trying to answer these latter questions can quickly create conflict. Well-meaning Christians can honestly arrive at different conclusions. Poverty is a multifaceted problem with no simple solutions, so political debates over how to reduce poverty will always be complex and often contentious.

An Overview of Poverty in the United States

Although poverty is a global issue, for the purpose of this discussion let's narrow our focus to domestic poverty. In the United States we attempt to measure poverty with a formula designed to calculate the money required to provide for basic human needs such as food, shelter, and clothing. Official government poverty statistics calculate how many households and people live on incomes below the estimated poverty threshold (also called the poverty line).[5] An estimated 46.2 million Americans, or 15.1 percent of the population, lived in poverty in 2010.[6]

From the time of the nation's founding until the Great Depression, the federal government provided very little direct help for society's poor. Churches and other charities did their best to meet the needs, while government largely stayed away. In the wake of the devastating poverty, hunger, and job losses during the Depression, President Franklin D. Roosevelt promoted widespread reforms that shifted the burden of care significantly (but not entirely) from private organizations to the federal government, ushering in the era of the so-called welfare state.

As the scope of government has expanded, so have programs to care for the poor and needy. Workers and their employers contribute to Social Security and unemployment insurance, which in turn provides benefits to retirees, the disabled, and the unemployed. Other assistance programs supplement the income of the poorest Americans by helping them purchase food and by providing low-cost housing or rent subsidies. Medicare and Medicaid provide health insurance to the elderly and the poor. By any measure, these and other related government programs reduce poverty and help meet basic human needs. The combined effects of safety-net programs kept an estimated 38 million Americans out of poverty in 2009.[7]

★ ★ ★

The debates about how to best care for the poor are not about *if* the government should provide assistance, but instead about *how much* and *in what form*.

★ ★ ★

Although one hears the occasional call for abandoning these and other safety-net programs, almost everyone accepts that they are now a permanent part of the American economy. Thus, the debates about how to best care for the poor are not about *if* the government should provide assistance, but instead about *how much* and *in what form*. The heart of current debates over poverty policy is thus about the best way to allocate scarce resources. Consider three examples of possible means to reduce the number of Americans living in poverty: cutting taxes to stimulate economic growth, increasing government spending on safety-net programs, and relying more on religious and community organizations to meet the needs of the poor.

Cutting Taxes to Stimulate the Economy

Many factors contribute to poverty, but one factor in particular provides a direct way to increase household income. Jobs are an important part of any poverty reduction program. As people find and retain jobs, they are better able to provide for themselves and their families, becoming more likely to move out of poverty.

Advocates of free-market economics support tax reduction as a way to stimulate the economy and create new jobs. The explanation goes something like this: High taxes and government regulations increase the costs of doing business. When individuals and businesses pay fewer taxes, they have more money available to spend and invest. Companies have more money available to pay their workers, so they may hire new employees. Individuals will use their increased spending power to buy more goods and services. Increased investment and increased consumer spending can lead to economic growth and more jobs.

The free-market think tank the Goldwater Institute analyzed Census Bureau poverty statistics from 1990–2000 and found a link between low taxes and poverty reduction. As the lead researcher summarized, their analysis "[demonstrates] that low-tax and -spending states enjoyed sizable decreases in poverty rates during the 1990s. High-tax and -spending states, meanwhile, suffered *increases* in poverty rates."[8] Although many factors besides taxation affect poverty rates, this and other similar studies provide support for proponents of tax cuts.

Yet critics are quick to note that tax cuts do not automatically create economic growth. A report by United for a Fair Economy, a progressive think tank, summarizes: "Tax cuts have sometimes been followed by periods of increased unemployment; at other times, tax cuts have been followed by sharp declines in unemployment. By the same token, tax increases have not always been followed by the doomsday predicted by conservatives."[9]

Do tax cuts have an independent effect on economic growth and job creation? Most (but not all) economists think so, but such direct cause-and-effect relationships are difficult, if not impossible, to measure.

Supporting Public Assistance Programs

Another possible method for combating poverty is expanding existing government programs that serve low-income Americans. Congress decides how much to spend on these and all other programs through what we call the budget process. Most federal dollars are spent automatically as determined by permanent law, but hundreds of billions of dollars remain to be divided among a wide scope of government agencies and activities.

Every year organizations descend upon Congress, lobbying legislators to allocate money for the programs they care about. Advocates for the poor vie for time with representatives from businesses, unions, trade associations, and other interest groups. Those who seek to reduce poverty by expanding public assistance programs must compete for scarce government resources with everyone else.

Activists who emphasize the need for public assistance programs often begin their advocacy by responding to the president's annual budget request, combing through the hundreds of pages to see how programs targeting the poor have fared. In recent years, some religious leaders have begun referring to government budgets as "moral documents," contending that fiscal priorities reflect the government's values. During the government standoff over deficit reduction in 2011, for example, leaders from fifty religious organizations circulated a letter to the president and members of Congress that concluded:

> Budgets are moral documents, and how we reduce future deficits are historic and defining moral choices. As Christian leaders, we urge Congress and the administration to give moral priority to programs that protect the life and dignity of poor and vulnerable people in these difficult times, our broken economy, and our wounded world. It is the vocation and obligation of the church to speak and act on behalf of those Jesus called "the least of these."[10]

From this vantage point, political leaders should place greatest budgetary priority on direct government aid to the poor.

Given the unwritten rules of budgetary politics, it is difficult to reduce taxes and increase spending on public assistance at the same time. To a large extent, therefore, the debate reflects ideological differences over the roles of government and the private sector. Those who support expanding assistance programs typically believe in a strong role for government, a hallmark of liberal ideology. On the other hand, those who advocate tax cuts are usually ideological conservatives who prefer more limited government. When reporters asked Tony Perkins, the president of the conservative Christian organization Family Research Council, why he wasn't joining religious protests against a budget proposal, he responded: "'There is a [biblical] mandate to take care of the poor. There is no dispute of that fact,' he said. 'But it does not say government should do it. That's a shifting of responsibility.'"[11]

Reliance on Religious and Community Groups That Serve the Poor

At the same time that liberals and conservatives debate the relative merits of tax policy and public assistance, another approach looks to religious and community organizations for help. Private charities undoubtedly play a significant role in meeting the needs of the poor.

In addition to the thousands of independent and congregation-based organizations across the country, large faith-based networks provide social services to tens of millions of Americans each year with funding from private and government sources. The Salvation Army serves about 33 million people each year, providing help such as emergency food and shelter, substance abuse treatment, and disaster relief. Catholic Charities, a network of social service agencies, spends over $2.5 billion each year to assist about 9 million people. Lutheran Services in America helps about 6 million people annually, providing a range of services including health care, housing, mental health, and emergency and disaster relief.

Some charities offer assistance to the poor, replacing services government might otherwise provide or helping the poor in ways that the government does not. In many instances, however, charities and government work together in partnership. Government agencies rarely provide services themselves; typically they contract with private and non-profit organizations that do the actual work. For example, the Department of Housing and Urban Development's Continuum of Care program provided $1.4 billion in 2010 to groups working to meet the needs of the homeless and those at risk of becoming homeless.[12] HUD does not operate its own homeless programs; instead, it gives grants to local organizations across the country.

THE STATISTICS WAR:
WHAT SHOULD YOU BELIEVE?

★ ★ ★

WHEN EVALUATING POLICY options, it makes sense to do comparative research. But what do you do when different studies seem to reach opposite conclusions? Which do you believe? As with any discernment process, there are no foolproof methods to identify what source is best. You can, however, ask a series of questions that can help you evaluate the relative strength and weakness of published reports and the organizations that release them.

- **Always read the fine print**, looking for disclaimers and other clues about the limitations and weaknesses of a study. Ask yourself: What, if anything, seems to be missing from the analysis? What questions didn't they ask? What findings and data do they minimize or downplay?
- **Realize you may be reading just one side of the story.** Advocacy groups in particular are famous for reporting incomplete data. Most organizations report what is technically true—their reputations are at risk if they lie. But they are likely to tell only one side of the story and exaggerate the effects of policy change. Ask yourself: Does this analysis make room for differing viewpoints or does it only represent one side of a policy debate? Are any of the findings negative? Do they make claims that seem particularly outlandish?
- **Evaluate the source of the information.** Who is reporting this information? Do they appear to rep

> resent a particular set of interests or perspectives? Who benefits from what they report? Who loses? Who paid for the study?
> - **Rely on multiple sources.** Compare what different people and groups say about a particular proposal.

Whether partnering with government or working independently, local charitable organizations contribute greatly to serving the poor. Churches, non-profits, and other groups in every community feed the hungry, shelter the homeless, train people for employment, teach English, and provide other tangible assistance that meets human needs.

★ ★ ★

Meeting immediate needs may be necessary,
but it will never be sufficient for solving poverty.

★ ★ ★

Then again, some observers note that charitable work is rarely enough to deal with the underlying problems of poverty. Distinguishing between the concepts of "charity" and "justice," one commentator explained: "It's the difference between running a soup kitchen to feed the hungry and working in the political system to change the policies that allow people to go hungry."[13] Meeting immediate needs may be necessary, but it will never be sufficient for solving poverty.

All or Nothing?

The examples described above are brief snapshots of some of the issues raised when comparing different ways to combat poverty. They are not necessarily mutually exclusive, for it is possible (and even customary) to pursue some or all of these policies at the same time. Standard political rhetoric often implies that one, and only one, particular proposal holds the key to caring for the poor. In reality, almost all social policy in the United States reflects a combination of government action and private assistance. It is widely accepted that the government should provide some basic safety net for the poorest and most vulnerable members of society, just as there is widespread agreement that religious and charitable organizations play a significant role in meeting human needs. The real arguments are at the margins over how much the government should do and in what ways private organizations should contribute. Christians with different ideological views will likely disagree about the answers.

Search for Common Ground, then Agree to Disagree

Returning yet again to the command to love God and neighbor, how might Christians respond to fellow believers who do not share their political views? How can we advocate our perspectives on policy in ways that honor those with whom we disagree?

A good place to start is searching for areas of agreement and acknowledging common ground. So many political debates are really about the best way to achieve a shared goal, yet much popular rhetoric ignores or distorts this reality. When beginning a political discussion, affirm one another's shared goals first and then talk about the disagreements over which policy—or policies!—will work best.

NAME CALLING, MOCKERY, AND OTHER INSULTS

★ ★ ★

IF YOU WONDER why it can be so difficult to disagree about politics respectfully, consider some of the titles of a few recent books on current affairs.

From conservative authors:

- **Arguing with Idiots**: *How to Stop Small Minds and Big Government*
- **Gangster Government**: *Barack Obama and the New Washington Thugocracy*
- **Demonic**: *How the Liberal Mob Is Endangering America*

From liberal authors:

- **Pitchforks and Torches**: *The Worst of the Worst, from Beck, Bill, and Bush to Palin and Other Posturing Republicans*
- **Wingnuts**: *How the Lunatic Fringe Is Hijacking America*
- **The Wrecking Crew**: *How Conservatives Ruined Government, Enriched Themselves, and Beggared the Nation*

When discussing policy alternatives with those who disagree, ask them questions to help you better understand their perspective and to learn more about their proposed solution. At the same time that you ask probing questions, be prepared to answer similar questions about your own positions and why you think they make sense. Consider some questions you might use to begin this conversation:

- Why do you believe that this particular solution is best?
- When did you first learn about this policy? What in particular captured your attention?
- What are the strengths and weaknesses of doing this?
- Has this solution been tried before? If so, what happened?
- What biblical principles inform your support for this policy alternative? What biblical principles potentially conflict with it?

By asking each other questions with a willingness to listen to other perspectives, we demonstrate love and respect, expanding opportunities to learn from one another.

Entering conversations with genuine humility can help you gain new insights into the many complexities of public policy. Talking with those who hold different political views may seem risky, for such discussions require us to challenge our presuppositions and ask questions of ourselves. But the rewards clearly outweigh the risks, for in facing tough conversations we learn from one another and about ourselves, gaining a richer understanding of multiple political perspectives and the reasons behind them.

Finally, and most importantly, we should make sure that our political differences do not hinder our fellowship with brothers and sisters in Christ. As Peter wrote to the early church: "The end of all things is near. Therefore be clear minded and self-controlled so that you can pray. Above all, love each other deeply, because love covers over a multitude of sins. Offer hospitality to one another without grumbling" (1 Peter 4:7–9). The unity of believers is of far greater scope and consequence than our disagreements over the best way to achieve political goals.

Having made it this far in this book, it is now time for you to apply what you have learned to political action. The next chapter offers practical steps to prepare you to vote. After explaining why the roles and duties of political office matter for voting, the chapter offers tips to help you order policy priorities, research and evaluate political candidates, and ultimately make an informed voting decision.

QUESTIONS FOR DISCUSSION

Reflecting

1. What are some of your first thoughts when you discover that a Christian friend holds a different political position than you?

2. What are some of the strengths and weaknesses of the different means of reducing poverty in the United States discussed in this chapter?

Responding

3. What can you do to encourage meaningful and respectful dialogue with those who do not share your political views?

Chapter 10

★ ★ ★

Ready, Set, Vote!
A Decision-Making Guide

The most important political office is that of the private citizen.

—LOUIS BRANDEIS

The best argument against democracy is a conversation with the average voter.

—WINSTON CHURCHILL

I have been fascinated by American politics most of my life. Early childhood memories include joining my mother in the voting booth, hiding with her behind the curtain, and watching her pull the levers to vote. In first grade, I entertained my friends with political impressions during recess. A few years later, I worked on the first of what would be many campaigns, helping deliver and set up yard signs for a family friend's state senate run. By the time I was in high school, I was volunteering on a phone bank for a presidential race. A photograph of me and a friend watching the returns at a presidential victory party made the front page of the local newspaper. I was fascinated to learn about political campaigns from the inside, and I eagerly awaited the first election when I would be old enough to vote.

I can still recall my excitement as I drove to the polling place to vote for the first time. My mood quickly dampened, however, when I entered the voting booth and was overcome by the long list of elected offices listed on the ballot. Some names I knew, so those votes were simple. But the list of candidates and offices was much longer than I had expected. I felt paralyzed, unsure of what to do. In the end, I left many of the boxes blank and exited the voting booth feeling like a failure.

Have you ever had a similar experience of feeling overwhelmed by a long and complicated ballot? With so many elections decided at once, it can seem impossible to learn enough about every race to feel prepared to vote. As we will see in this chapter, however, it is indeed possible to learn enough about the candidates to make an informed decision. After looking at some of the different ways that people view representation, we'll consider some questions you can ask and point you to resources that will help you find answers as you evaluate political candidates and get ready to vote.

The Expectations Game: Theories of Representation

In a representative democracy like the United States, citizens vote to elect people to office who they believe will work on our behalf in government. Political theorists often talk about two common models of representation: delegate and trustee. According to the *delegate model*, elected officials represent their constituents by directly reflecting their desires and opinions. As delegates for the people, the primary job of elected officials is to determine what the majority of their constituents want and translate these desires into public policy. An alternative view of representation, the *trustee model*, expects elected officials to draw upon their knowledge and experience to make decisions that they believe are in the best interests of their constituents. Since voters rarely have enough information or expertise to know what is best, they choose to place their trust in someone with specific skills and knowledge to act on their behalf.

Although these two models appear to be opposites, in practice, voters seem to expect their representatives to somehow serve as both delegates and trustees. Most candidates make early appeals to voters following the trustee model: they introduce themselves to voters by stressing their background, expertise, and character. In later campaign ads, candidates focus more on their role as delegates, taking sides on heated issues and showing how they contrast with their opponents. Data from post-election polls suggest that voters base their decisions both on their perception of candidate character and the policy issues they advocate.

Once in office, elected officials seem to serve as delegates on some issues and trustees on others. Recent research on the House of Representatives suggests that members are more likely to think of themselves as delegates on economic and domestic policy but feel more freedom to "vote their conscience" and serve as trustees on so-called moral issues such as abortion and gay rights.[1]

When making a voting decision, evaluate candidates with your preferred model of representation in mind. If you generally follow the delegate model, choose the candidate who seems most responsive to voter concerns and most likely to vote with the constituents regardless of the issue. In contrast, if you are most concerned that an officeholder is trustworthy to make decisions on your behalf, you should primarily evaluate candidates based on their background, expertise, and perceived character.

Before You Enter the Voting Booth: Ways to Prepare

Once you have an idea of the type of representative you think would be best, what else should you do to prepare for Election Day? Before choosing among candidates, first decide which political issues matter the most to you and learn more about the different positions on the ballot.

Priorities, Priorities

Given the diversity of issues raised in a political campaign and the even wider range of topics elected officials are likely to consider over the course of a term in office, it seems impossible to find any candidate with whom you will agree completely. With this in mind, which issues should be most important when choosing which person to support?

Some voters answer this question by selecting one issue they believe is most important and evaluating candidates based on it. We call this *single issue voting.* If you are so passionate about a particular issue that you believe it always outweighs other policies an elected official must address while in office, single issue voting makes sense.

In practice, however, single issue voting rarely works. Sometimes political opponents agree. If your single issue is low taxes and both candidates pledge not to increase taxes, you cannot choose between them. In other cases, the role and duties of office may have little or nothing to do with the identified issue. If your single issue is pacifism, for example, you can likely make a wise choice between candidates for Congress, but the issue will be of little use when voting for county clerk.

★ ★ ★

In practice single issue
voting rarely works.

★ ★ ★

Most voters decide it is best to evaluate candidates on the basis of several issues at the same time, so they need to find ways to prioritize what issues matter most to them. One method is to determine *non-negotiable issues*, those policy positions (if any) that are so important that a candidate must share your views on them to earn your vote. If issues are truly non-negotiable, skip voting in those races where neither candidate shares your views. Yet another approach is to create a list of your *priority issues*, those issues that you believe are most important for each elected office, and choose the candidate whose positions on these issues are closest to yours.

Much like the nature of politics itself, weighing the importance of issues and selecting a candidate among imperfect choices requires a delicate balancing act and will likely require compromise. There is no perfect formula for choosing a candidate; even as a professional political scientist, I have found an occasional voting decision so difficult that I have intentionally chosen no one. If you enter the voting booth and don't feel comfortable with your choices for an office, leave it blank and cast your vote in the other races on the ballot.

Evaluating the Roles and Duties of Office

After you are comfortable with how to prioritize issues that matter most to you, it helps to find out what races are on the ballot in a given election. Once you know what offices are contested, learn more about the principal duties and powers of each office. Evaluate candidates much like an employer would screen résumés when filling a job opening, thinking first about the particular qualifications and background that seem most relevant for the job. All things being equal, it makes sense that candidates for district attorney would be lawyers with experience in trial courts, that a prospective sheriff have law enforcement experience, and that a state treasurer have a background in finance or accounting.

Look also at the duties and powers of office to determine the issues the elected official is most likely to influence. As you weigh the relative merits of competing candidates, consider their positions on issues most related to the particular offices they seek and then determine whose views are closest to yours on those issues. Consider a few examples. A school board member has significant power over budgets and curriculum at local public schools, so pay particular attention to each candidate's views on education and fiscal responsibility. A sheriff has great influence over criminal investigations and law enforcement, so compare the candidates' statements about their priorities for running the sheriff's department.

Getting to Yes: Learning about Candidates and Campaigns

Voter education is at the same time one of the easiest and one of the hardest aspects of making a voting decision. As an election nears, campaign stories dominate news coverage and political appeals flood the airwaves, mailboxes, and phone lines. It often seems impossible to ignore the upcoming election. Is it possible to learn anything useful in the midst of such chaos? Although campaigns can be frustrating and confusing, with a bit of persistence you can learn a lot about the candidates for office to make your voting decisions easier.

Information Overload? Campaign News

In the era of modern campaigning, it is all but impossible to avoid seeing some form of campaign communications during a hotly contested election. The media strategy for almost all political campaigns is the same: maximize coverage in the news while targeting voters with as much paid advertising as your budget will allow.

Candidates and their campaign staff make many efforts to draw attention to their campaigns and encourage news coverage. One common strategy is sending *press releases*, prefabricated news stories that alert the media to events and issues of concern to the campaign and provide ready-made content that journalists can quote freely. Another common tactic for attracting free media is scheduling events with high-profile guests. When the president of the United States or a well-known rock star campaigns for a candidate, journalists take notice.

★ ★ ★

An interesting irony of campaigning
is that bad news is almost always
better than no news at all.

★ ★ ★

Although candidates work hard to receive positive media coverage, an interesting irony of campaigning is that bad news is almost always better than no news at all. Many voters, often unknowingly, determine a candidate's chance of winning in part from the amount of media coverage the campaign receives. If the news media never mention a particular candidate, voters assume he has no chance. If stories about a candidate appear with regularity, voters believe she can win. Since volume of media coverage can signal voters in this way, campaigns typically prefer negative news coverage to none at all. Obviously, a candidate is more likely to lose if journalists only report bad news, but a mixture of negative and positive media coverage typically helps a candidate.

News media reports are an important source of information useful for comparing candidates. Stories about campaign events are often the least informative; candidate profiles and broadcast debates usually offer the most details. The evening network news programs always cover presidential races and occasionally run a short story on a particularly competitive congressional or gubernatorial race, but, for the most part, local news stations will be the best broadcast sources for regular updates on state and local races. Because newspapers and news websites have much more space to tell a story than traditional television or radio broadcasts, these sources are likely to offer the most frequent and most detailed coverage of state and local elections.

In the weeks and days preceding an election, newspaper editorial boards often offer candidate endorsements. Although the political slant of the editorial page is usually well known (before its 2008 endorsement of Barack Obama, for example, the *Chicago Tribune* had last endorsed a Democratic presidential candidate in 1872), endorsements can provide insights into contested races and help voters make a final decision.

Can You Learn Anything Useful from Campaign Ads?

Even as campaigns work hard to attract media coverage, they allocate most of their budgets for paid media. Candidates want to control the content of their communication as much as possible, and they craft messages to appeal both to broad and narrow groups of voters.

Candidates need to build their name recognition with the voters, so basic advertising is essential. Most campaigns begin with a simple logo, commonly some combination of patriotic red, white, and blue with the name of the candidate and the office sought. This logo will appear in many forms—in signs dotting neighborhood lawns, in banner ads on the side of city buses or pasted across billboards, as stickers affixed to car bumpers and windows, and on T-shirts of college students. Simple logos communicate very little about the candidate, but the combined effect of thousands of stickers, signs, and billboards viewed for many months can create a lasting impression.

Other forms of general campaign communication include brochures and door knockers, tri-fold or single page ads briefly describing the candidate's background and issue positions. Usually full color and often including a cheerful family photo, brochures are typically printed in mass quantities for general distribution at events and for candidates and campaign workers to leave on doors when walking through neighborhoods. As such, these ads rarely highlight controversial issues but instead list uncontroversial accomplishments and include promises designed to have broad appeal. General campaign literature typically provides very few details to help you make a voting decision.

HOW MUCH DO CAMPAIGNS COST?

★ ★ ★

HAVE YOU EVER WONDERED how much candidates spend on their campaigns? The 2008 presidential election broke all previous records, as the two major party candidates spent more than $1 billion. In 2010, candidates for the 435 seats in the House of Representatives raised almost $1.1 billion. The average House race cost $570,000. Candidates for the 37 open seats in the United States Senate spent a combined total of $745 million. The average Senate race cost $2.4 million. Where does all that money go? The typical campaign devotes about two thirds of its spending to voter contact, with most of that money paying for advertisements.

The most pointed and focused campaign messages appear in targeted communications, those ads designed to connect with a particular segment of the voting public. In direct mail pieces, campaigns send large postcards or fold-out brochures, often with sinister photographs and dire warnings, to selected groups deemed likely to resonate with the message. A candidate who favors gun control, for example, might target direct mailings to mothers of young children, using pictures of automatic rifles and small children on a playground to warn against his opponent's lax policies on assault weapons. Direct mail pieces often rely on emotional appeals and exaggeration; such ads rarely offer enough information to educate voters but commonly spread rumors and distortions.

Campaigns also target voters in radio ads. Because radio stations offer a wide variety of formats, candidates can tailor ads to the likely concerns of the listeners. A candidate reaching out for the Latino vote might run an ad on a Spanish-language station; a candidate hoping to appeal to younger voters may advertise on a rock station. Although limited to 15, 30, or 60 seconds, these advertisements can provide some useful information about a candidate's background or issue stances.

One of the most visible forms of paid media, television advertisements, is typically a factor in just a small number of political contests. Only the highest profile campaigns—president, governor, Congress, and some statewide offices—are likely to have the budget and geographical reach to make television spots feasible.

Television commercials can help inform voters, but they are also likely to create distorted views of the candidates. Clever media consultants comb through voting records, finding ways to make the most reasoned and careful legislator appear sinister or bizarre. If you think an ad makes a claim that sounds preposterous or exaggerated, in most cases your instincts are probably right. Instead of accepting an ad's message at face value, do further research to make sure the information is truthful.

Although there is no perfect formula for evaluating the content of broadcast commercials, tools such as "ad-watches," media stories that evaluate the truthfulness of campaign advertising claims, can help voters separate truth from distortion. Watchdog websites like factcheck.org and politifact.com monitor the accuracy of political speeches and advertisements, providing searchable databases for testing the truth of campaign claims.

To add further confusion to the communications blitz common in the campaign season, political parties and outside groups run their own advertisements in high-profile, high-stakes political contests. Groups that have an interest in the outcome of an election can advertise openly as long as they do not coordinate their efforts with any candidate's campaign and they comply with campaign finance laws. The rules, regulations, and terminology affecting outside groups and political campaigns are complex and constantly changing. From the vantage point of a prospective voter, perhaps it is most important to be aware that organizations beyond the individual candidates and their campaigns can and do try to influence election results.

When evaluating information in campaign ads, check to see the source of the material. Because candidates are directly accountable for the claims that they make in their campaign communications, official campaign sources are more likely than those created by outside groups to provide accurate information about a candidate's views.

Researching Candidates on Your Own

All of the resources we've discussed so far can help you learn about candidates for office, but what are ways you can do your own research to prepare for an election? An excellent place to start is at each candidate's campaign website. Using your favorite Internet search engine, locate these websites. If you don't know the names of all of the candidates, most county political parties provide links from their official sites. As you would expect, campaign websites are one-sided and portray candidates as positively as possible, but they can be valuable resources. You can learn a lot about candidates' priorities by seeing what content they display most prominently and what issues are of such low priority that they receive no mention at all.

Interest group websites are another useful source of information. Many groups design particular tools to educate voters. Some organizations calculate *ratings* that evaluate candidates currently in office, listing the most important votes related to issues they advocate and calculating the percentage of times the legislator votes with the organization. The U.S. Chamber of Commerce, for example, compiles ratings based on pro-business votes, ranging from a score of 100 indicating voting with the Chamber on every vote measured, to a score of 0 for those who never voted with the Chamber. Interest group ratings are biased by design; that is, they indicate how closely a legislator votes with the organization's policy agenda. If you are a member of an interest group or simply find yourself supportive of its views, checking to see if it rates voting records may help you evaluate the performance of candidates running for re-election or who currently hold legislative office.

INTEREST GROUPS AND VOTING RECORDS

★ ★ ★

MANY INTEREST GROUPS keep track of legislators' votes on issues of likely importance to their members. Here are a few examples:

American Association of Retired Persons
(www.aarp.org) — AARP is the largest interest group in the United States. Open to adults age 50 and over, the group monitors issues of likely concern to older

Americans. Check out their summary of key votes of interest and links to state fact sheets: http://www.aarp.org/politics-society/advocacy/key_vote_summary/.

U.S. Chamber of Commerce (www.uschamber.com) — This federation of more than 3 million businesses is the most prominent voice representing business interests in Washington. Visit their links to past editions of How They Voted, a list of pro-business votes compiled by the Chamber: http://www.uscham ber.com/issues/legislators/how-they-voted.

Family Research Council (www.frc.org) — The FRC is a conservative, faith-based group that highlights "family values" issues. Find their interactive map with links to congressional scorecards at http://www.frcaction.org/scorecard.

League of Conservation Voters (www.lcv.org) — The LCV is a national organization that advocates for environmental conservation. You can access their national environmental scorecard, which includes key votes as well as reports on committee and party leaders, at http://www.lcv.org/scorecard/.

National Right to Life Committee (www.nrlc.org) — The NRLC is a national organization that raises awareness of a range of pro-life issues. Their legislative action center offers commentary on current political issues and links to NRLC scorecards of key votes on right to life issues: http://www.capwiz.com/nrlc/home/.

Before each election some interest groups create *voter guides*, side-by-side comparisons of major party candidates on selected issues. Although groups may say the guides are non-partisan, organizations choose issues that fit with their mission and values. As such, most voter guides favor candidates of the party most closely aligned with the organization's mission. One of the most famous organizations to issue voter guides, the Christian Coalition, offers this typical disclaimer: "This voter guide is provided for educational purposes only and is not to be construed as an endorsement of any candidate or party." On the ten votes listed in their 2010 Senate election guide, however, the Coalition was consistently on the side of Republicans.[2]

★ ★ ★

One of the most important (and often overlooked) sources of voter education is conversation with friends and family.

★ ★ ★

Other resources are available that provide more balanced information on political candidates. Several non-partisan organizations compile information to help voters make side-by-side candidate comparisons on a broader range of issues. One of the oldest and most respected of these groups, the League of Women Voters, provides local voter education through projects such as newspaper inserts with candidate information and sponsoring candidate debates. The organization's website (www.vote411.org) provides information on voter registration, polling times and places, and candidates and ballot issues. The League sends questionnaires to candidates and compiles the responses. Another reliable voter education group, Project Vote Smart (www.votesmart.org; 1-888-VOTE-SMART), collects and reports candidate responses to surveys about salient political issues. Their website also provides a wealth of data on most candidates including biographical information, campaign finance reports, voting records, interest group ratings, and links to public speeches.

Although outside resources can be quite useful to raise voter awareness, one of the most important (and often overlooked) sources of voter education is conversation with friends and family. From casual conversations about the latest television ads to discussions about how candidates performed in a debate, at least some people you know are likely to talk about upcoming elections. Those who follow politics most closely are apt to initiate conversations about candidates and public policy; those who are less familiar with politics may want to ask family and friends to explain how they are planning to vote and why. Such conversations, particularly with people you trust who follow a wide range of news sources, might offer a low-pressure environment for asking questions and formulating opinions.

Volunteering for Campaigns

As you learn about different candidates and the policies they support, you may decide that you want to help with a campaign. Most political campaigns can only afford to pay a few staff members, so they rely heavily on volunteers to help with a range of tasks such as contacting voters, staffing events, preparing mailings, and, on the day of the election, calling likely supporters to remind them to vote. If you discover a candidate whom you want to help, call or email the campaign office and let them know your availability. In all likelihood, they will put you to work quickly. Those who don't have much time to volunteer can still attend a campaign event to demonstrate support and to learn more about the candidate's issue positions.

You can also show your support by donating to campaigns or to interest groups that raise issues that are important to you. Candidates rely on donations to get their message to voters; it is almost impossible to win without a well-funded campaign.

Ready, Set, Vote!

Although the idea of voting sounds simple enough, the actual practice of deciding how to vote can be quite complicated. With more than half a million elected officials, the United States has far more elections than any other country in the world and, therefore, demands the most from its voters. This chapter has provided tools and suggestions to make you more comfortable and better equipped the next time you vote.

Christians can and should exercise their right to vote; free elections are essential to a vibrant democracy. But voting is just one of many options for participating in government. In the next chapter, we will explore some additional ways your faith can inform politics, offering practical suggestions for how to get involved in the political process. We'll conclude with some final thoughts to keep in mind as you seek to honor God in politics.

QUESTIONS FOR DISCUSSION

Reflecting

1. Would you rather your elected representatives function more as delegates or more as trustees? Why?
2. What political issues are most important to you? How did you reach this conclusion?

Responding

3. What resources will be most helpful to you as you decide if and how to vote? How can you help prepare others for Election Day?

Chapter 11

★ ★ ★

Honoring God in Politics: Where Do We Go from Here?

If your heart is in the right place and you have good taste, not only will you pass muster in politics, you are destined for it. If you are modest and do not lust after power, not only are you suited to politics, you absolutely belong there.

—VÁCLAV HAVEL

Growing up in West Texas, football was a part of my life as long as I can remember. Thanksgiving meals began before the kick-off of the Dallas Cowboys' game; we waited until halftime for pecan pie and other desserts. Beginning when I was in elementary school, my family attended high school football games almost every Friday night. I have spent many Sunday afternoons watching the NFL, following my favorite teams and players. Live or on television, I love the seemingly constant motion and action of the game.

Baseball, however, was another story. For much of my life I could not understand why anyone would watch such a boring game on television. I enjoyed attending the occasional live game, but the appeal was not the game itself as much as it was the excitement of the crowd, the obligatory hot dog, Coke, and peanuts, and the chance to share an adventure with family or friends. Today, I am a genuine baseball fan. I eagerly await the start of baseball season so I can once again watch my beloved White Sox. I follow the team with interest and look forward to watching games on television. The game of baseball did not change, but what I once found boring I now find exciting. What happened that transformed my perspective? The answer is simple: I learned the game. Before I understood the game well, I watched baseball in anticipation of exciting offense, waiting for what often seemed a long time for something interesting to happen. But I now understand that the game is much more about pitching and defense than it is about hitting the ball. I still love watching a player hit a home run deep into the stands, but I find it even more exciting to watch a no-hitter in progress, biting my nails in anticipation that no one will succeed against my pitcher. Now that I understand the game better and know *how* to watch baseball, I enjoy it as much as, if not more than, football.

Following politics is a lot like following baseball. The more you understand the rules of the game, the more fascinating it becomes.

In many ways, following politics is a lot like following baseball. The more you understand the rules of the game, the more fascinating it becomes. Waiting for the government to take a final action can seem to take forever. But as your vantage point changes, you may develop an interest in watching politicians design a campaign game plan, respond to attacks, and forge winning coalitions. You may also see your role transform as well. As you learn more about current events and the work of government, you may find yourself wanting to do more than watch. No longer content to just sit in the stands, you now want to participate more actively in the political process and try to change the game itself.

Would you like to have a greater voice in politics? Are you interested in finding new ways to make a difference? This final chapter will help you in these tasks, pointing you to tools to help you follow politics more closely, engage with governmental leaders on issues of concern, and reach out to care for those in need. We'll begin with a discussion of ways you can make a difference individually and through the church before concluding with some final thoughts on how we can honor God in politics.

The Best Participant Is an Informed Participant

The first and likely best step to help you get more involved in politics is educating yourself about political issues, current events, and government. You have already begun this task by reading this book. To continue your political education, follow news coverage from a range of reputable sources.

Most Americans learn about politics and current events from the news media. Those who are best informed gather information from a combination of newspaper, television, radio, and Internet sources. It helps to pay attention to straight news coverage (stories that describe events by answering who, what, when, where, and how questions) as well as opinion and commentary (stories that express a particular point of view). Although it requires significant time and effort, getting news from a diverse range of sources will increase your understanding of the complexity of political issues and better prepare you to apply your faith to politics.

Even in today's constantly changing media environment, the newspaper remains one of the best places to find political news. Newspapers employ large staffs of reporters and editors who prepare a wide range of stories and offer some of the broadest coverage and most detailed information available to the public. Whether you are concerned about the impact of local budget cuts or want to follow the latest debate on Capitol Hill, newspapers provide current information on a range of political topics. Their online editions update content day and night, providing almost instant access to the latest developments.

Political websites that provide access to commentary, original reporting, and links to other stories of likely interest are also useful sources. One of the best resources for straight news is Politico.com, the website arm of a Washington, D.C.-area media organization devoted entirely to politics. Many other political websites have found a following by offering a particular ideological angle. A few popular sites with a liberal bent are Dailykos.com, talking pointsmemo.com, and HuffingtonPost.com. For a more conservative slant, consider visiting dailycaller.com, realclearpolitics.com, or powerline.com. Watchblog.com, a multi-perspective site with three editors, provides commentary and links to content representing Democratic, Republican, and Independent perspectives. Two other helpful blogs are globalvoices.org, a website that compiles reports from blogs around the world, and propublica.org, an investigative journalism website.

Whatever media outlets you choose to follow, don't limit yourself exclusively to those sources that tell you what you want to hear. Studies confirm that people who only pay attention to sources that reinforce their political views are less informed and more likely to confuse facts and opinion. At its best, ideological commentary can help you learn about politics, but it won't help you understand multiple sides of an issue. If you regularly watch Fox News, turn the channel to MSNBC from time to time. If you get most of your news from liberal sources, pay attention to conservative outlets as well to broaden your knowledge and introduce you to alternative perspectives.

WEBSITES TO HELP YOU DIG DEEPER

★ ★ ★

THE INTERNET OFFERS many resources to help you learn more about political issues and connect you with elected officials. Here are a few examples of websites worth visiting:

- **Congress.org:** If you want to contact elected officials, type in your zip code on the home page to link to contact information for your state and federal elected officials. The site also includes links to legislative voting records, information about key legislation facing Congress, and a forum for debate.
- **www.opensecrets.org:** Run by the Center for Responsive Politics, this is a great resource to learn about money and politics in federal elections. You can quickly find information on campaign finance law, campaign spending, and who donates to whom.
- **American Enterprise Institute (www.aei.org):** AEI is a well-respected conservative "think tank," an organization that funds public policy research and hosts events.
- **Brookings Institution (www.brookings.edu):** Brookings is a well-respected liberal think tank that also helps inform public policy dialogue.

Making Your Voice Heard:
Interacting with Government

As you learn more about politics in the news, you may want to interact more with government. How do you make your voice heard? In most cases, the best way to make a difference in politics is to follow the activities of elected representatives and communicate with them when needed.

Watching Government in Action

Instead of relying solely on media sources to tell you what is happening, you can also watch governmental leaders at work. Elected officials hold public meetings to discuss issues, debate alternatives, and vote. If you turn to cable channels C-SPAN or C-SPAN 2 on weekdays, you are likely to see the House of Representatives or the Senate in action. These channels broadcast open committee sessions in which members gather to discuss and revise legislative proposals, and they show activity on the floor of each chamber. Although legislative business rarely makes for riveting television, anyone with access to cable television or the Internet can follow events as they happen.

The format varies somewhat across the country, but almost all local governing boards and commissions hold regularly scheduled meetings. If you want to watch them at work, visit your city or town website to find out when and where different boards and commissions meet and if they broadcast meetings on a local access channel. As the date of an event nears, websites will generally announce the agenda. If you hear that the local schools are considering changing the curriculum or that the city council is planning to close a railroad crossing you use daily, you may want to attend and share your concerns.

Lessons from history suggest that those
who are not responsive to constituent
needs often lose re-election.

★ ★ ★

The Power of the Pen: Contacting Elected Officials

Yet another way to make your voice heard is to contact legislators and other policy makers to express your views. Faxes, letters sent via email or traditional mail, posts on social networking sites, and phone calls are all ways to connect elected officials and their constituents, so most elected officials pay attention to them. Members of Congress, for example, take correspondence quite seriously; lessons from history suggest that those who are not responsive to constituent needs often lose re-election.

Because elected officials rarely have the time to read and reply to correspondence directly, most rely on their staff to manage communications and report on what constituents are saying. On especially contentious issues or those when an upcoming vote looks close, some legislators actually compare the volume of "pro" and "con" feedback to determine how to vote. Such communication gives policymakers an opportunity to hear from multiple vantage points and may persuade them to take action.

NOT ALL LETTERS ARE CREATED EQUAL: CONTACTING ELECTED OFFICIALS

★ ★ ★

BEFORE CONTACTING AN elected official with your concerns, consider a few pointers to maximize your influence and minimize your frustration.

- **Whenever possible, compose your own letter.** Nothing compares to a personal letter sent through the mail. Letters obviously written by individuals expressing their personal opinions matter most and almost always receive replies.
- **Elected officials may or may not pay attention to mass mailings.** Some people receive pre-printed postcards from interest groups that they sign and send to their legislators. Some offices will enter the information from such contacts, others will not. To maximize your influence, use such form letters and postcards as guides to write a letter in your own words.
- **If you email, you may or may not get a response.** Email is one of the quickest and easiest forms of contact, which means that offices get flooded with emails. Some legislators track all emails and reply to them, while others only send automated responses. As a general rule, for example, the White House does not send specific responses to emails.
- **When contacting an elected official for help with a government agency, call their local office.** Most elected officials have designated staff who are there to help constituents with a range of problems. Call and talk directly with a caseworker; you're likely to get more immediate response to a phone call than a letter.

Constituents also communicate with elected officials when they have problems with government agencies. Much of the work in the local offices of federal and state legislators involves responding to such requests. Caseworkers for U.S. senators and representatives can help people with problems such as navigating the immigration process, receiving their veterans' benefits, or finding a missing Social Security payment. In the same way, state legislators assist constituents with state benefits and programs. When someone calls from a congressional or state legislative office to request help, government agencies often respond quickly.

Participation in and through the Church

Participation in a local church offers yet another way to make a difference. Even those who have little interest in politics can show love for God and neighbor through churches and the organizations they support.

Church and community-based programs provide what is likely the best way to meet the specific needs of people near them. Some congregations serve the poor and needy through on-site programs; many others partner in the outreach efforts of nearby churches or local organizations. Anyone can help by donating time, money, goods, or services. Job training, food banks, and English as a second language classes are just a few examples of programs that depend on donations and volunteers.

It's surprisingly easy to connect with organizations that need your help. Church bulletins and newsletters often include announcements of service opportunities; pastors and priests can easily connect you with church programs and local organizations that provide a wide range of services. Although almost all organizations need regular volunteers, most also offer one-time or short-term opportunities to help. Many projects let families, small groups, or groups of friends and coworkers volunteer together.

Adult education classes and topical small groups offer additional ways to raise political awareness within your congregation. Consider teaching or organizing a non-partisan election-year class or group that encourages scriptural reflections, prayer for political leaders, and analysis of current events from a Christian perspective. If you don't feel equipped to facilitate such a class or group, attend one and participate in the discussion.

Christian Witness in Word and Deed

Having discussed some tools available to help you learn more about politics and better prepare you for political engagement, we now turn to a final and most important question. How can we make a distinctive difference as followers of Christ? Many well-meaning people are active in politics. Some are motivated by faith in Christ, others by different religions, and still others by a general sense of civic duty. But those of us who publicly profess Christianity are called to the higher standard of extending love to God and neighbor as witnesses of the gospel.

★ ★ ★

Political engagement is not ultimately about winning or losing; it is one way that God gives us to obey His commands and demonstrate His love to others.

★ ★ ★

And so we return once again to Paul's words in 1 Corinthians 12 and 13 and his reminder of the centrality of love as a guiding principle for life in community. Knowing that we only see as in a mirror dimly, we must always remember that we won't have all of the answers, nor do we need to pretend that we do. We can trust God and serve Him with humility. Political engagement is not ultimately about winning or losing; it is one way that God gives us to obey His commands and demonstrate His love to others. The central assumption of this book is that those involved in politics should work together in humility and with respect. Christians interacting in politics should avoid speaking with hate and hyperbole, committing instead to model Christ's love. The political arena may be one of the few places where many people outside the church interact with Christian believers. Our words, actions, and demeanor when advocating for political issues and candidates are an important part of our public witness for or against following Christ.

As part of that witness we should model a different kind of politics, one that invites conversation and transformation instead of condemnation of the other side. It is difficult but possible to implement a political strategy based upon the premises of presenting each side's political positions fairly and clearly, raising honest differences where they exist, and fostering open dialogue about different means to achieve policy goals. Such an approach undoubtedly runs counter to almost all of the norms of contemporary politics, but following Christ is by definition countercultural. Demonstrating Christian character in politics may not be a winning strategy in today's political climate, but political success should never be our end goal.

We must always keep our focus on the larger goals and purposes motivating our work and actions. Power is incredibly seductive— it can transform us rather than society. Once in the spotlight and in the corridors of power, it is very easy to lose sight of the principles and values that originally motivated our actions. Christians in politics need to hold one another accountable so they can avoid the many potential dangers and remain focused on serving God first.

Entering the Political Arena: Some Final Thoughts

As we have seen on our journey together, Christians can interact with and seek to influence government in many different ways. Because government has such a profound influence on society, many Christians will choose to engage in politics as one means of demonstrating love for God and neighbor. If you follow this path, here are some final thoughts to keep in mind that may promote respectful and fruitful political engagement.

• **Politics is complex.**
Government has already solved those problems that are easy to fix. Almost all of the issues that remain for public debate are complex and multifaceted. Accept the complexity of the process. Ask hard questions of anyone who proposes a quick fix or simple solution—sometimes creative people find new and simple ways to address policy issues, but most options that seem to offer an "easy way out" are actually too good to be true.

• **Expect compromise.**
By design, government depends on compromise and bargaining. Representatives bring a diversity of views, interests, and concerns to the table, so the political arena rarely, if ever, brings people to consensus. If you seek change through the political process, look for ways to encourage small changes that move in the right direction. On those issues where you cannot compromise, seek non-political solutions first.

• **Prepare yourself before entering public policy debates.**
Separate the goals you hope to achieve from the many different potential methods of achieving them. Seek agreement where possible, and determine the areas where disagreement will be inevitable. When debating means of achieving shared goals, be prepared to discuss many sides of the issue. Do your

homework so you can advocate your position with clarity, detail, and precision. Seek opportunities to learn from and engage in conversation with people representing other viewpoints.

• **Don't expect government to fix everything.**
Since government is in the business of addressing problems that are difficult (if not impossible) to solve, political solutions often only scratch the surface of a complex issue and leave many aspects unsolved. Representative government is only one of many institutions that pursue the common good.

• **Look to institutions outside of politics to help address problems.**
Politics is not the only way to achieve change. Churches, families, schools, faith-based and community organizations, and others play important roles in meeting people's needs and addressing problems. Seek ways that your church can care for those in need. Model Christian values in your family, and set a positive example for others.

• **Respect and honor your elected officials.**
Elected officials face many pressures, often work grueling schedules, and make significant sacrifices to enter public life. Although some politicians abuse their power, most are dedicated public servants trying to do their best to make a difference. Share your views with your political leaders; let them know when you respectfully disagree, and commend those whose actions you support.

• **Pray with sincerity.**
Most people are quick to criticize political leaders whose decisions they do not support; we should be even quicker to lift

them and their decisions to God in prayer. Although other more visible forms of political participation are important, nothing can replace the centrality of prayer.

As we have seen throughout this book, the structure and functions of American government are quite complicated, and political change is far from quick and easy. Political work requires determination, focus, and much perseverance. Christians who want to serve God in government will face many challenges, but they can also reap kingdom rewards. Our nation and our world need more committed Christians willing and able to participate in politics as a means of demonstrating God's love and mercy. Together we can offer a positive witness for the gospel as we honor God in politics.

QUESTIONS FOR DISCUSSION

Reflecting

1. What sources help you learn about political issues, current events, and government? What additional resources discussed in this chapter might help you learn more?

2. What would you most like to tell or ask the president? A member of Congress? A local governmental official?

Responding

3. Look over the list of final thoughts listed at the end of the chapter. How might these ideas and suggestions help you honor God in politics?

★ ★ ★

Notes

Chapter 1: Let's Talk! Bringing the Taboo to the Table

1. Colin Smith, *The Ten Greatest Struggles of Your Life* (Chicago: Moody, 2006), 49.
2. David E. Garland, "1 Corinthians," in *Dictionary for Theological Interpretation of the Bible*, ed. Kevin Vanhoozer (Grand Rapids, MI: Baker Academic, 2005), 133.
3. "Manchin Admits Mistakes and Apologizes," December 21, 2010, West Virginia Metro News, http://www.wvmetronews.com/index.cfm?func=displayfullstory&storyid=42054; and Lawrence Messina, "Sen. Manchin apologizes for missing weekend votes," December 21, 2010, Associated Press.
4. C. S. Lewis, *God in the Dock* (Grand Rapids, MI: Eerdmans, 1970), 198.

Chapter 2: Getting to Yes: The Perils and Promises of Religion and Politics

1. Quoted in William Martin, *With God on Our Side* (New York: Broadway, 1996), 171–72.
2. Stephen Monsma and Mark Rodgers, "In the Arena: Practical Issues in Concrete Political Engagement," in *Toward an Evangelical Public Policy*, eds. Ronald J. Sider and Diane Knippers (Grand Rapids, MI: Baker Books, 2005), 335.

Chapter 3: Is Government the Solution or the Problem? Its Purpose and Limits

1. Douglas L. Koopman, ed., *Serving the Claims of Justice: The Thoughts of Paul B. Henry* (Grand Rapids, MI: Paul B. Henry Institute, 2001), 261.

Chapter 4: Who Runs the Show? The Roles of Local, State, and Federal Government

1. Kristen Schorsch, "Tiny Taxing Districts with Limited Duties Scattered Across Illinois," *Chicago Tribune*, June 20, 2011, A1.
2. Data retrieved from the Cook County government website, http://blog.cookcountygov.com/.
3. For an insider look at the legislative process, see Amy E. Black, *From Inspiration to Legislation: How an Idea Becomes a Bill* (Upper Saddle River, NJ: Pearson Prentice Hall, 2007).

4. Edward S. Corwin, *The President: Office and Powers* (New York: New York University Press, 1940), 1.

5. Court Statistics Project, "State Court Caseload Statistics: An Analysis of 2008 State Court Caseloads" (Williamsburg, VA: National Center for State Courts, 2010), accessed July 12, 2011, http://www.ncsconline.org/ D_Research/csp/2008_files/Trial_Court_Tables.pdf.

6. William Martin, *With God on Our Side* (New York: Broadway, 1996), 384.

Chapter 5: Left, Right, or Center: Party, Ideology, and Politics

1. Barbara Sinclair. "Hostile Partners: The President, Congress, and Lawmaking in the Partisan 1990s," in *Polarized Politics: Congress and the President in a Partisan Era*, eds. Jon R. Bond and Richard Fleisher (Washington, D.C.: Congressional Quarterly Press, 2000), 137–40.

2. Professor Vanderbei displays his electoral maps and answers to frequently asked questions on his website: http://www.princeton.edu/~rvdb/JAVA/ election2008/.

3. John Danforth, *Faith and Politics* (New York: Viking, 2006), 10.

Chapter 6: Church, State, and the United States

1. Americans United for Separation of Church and State, "Is America a 'Christian Nation'? Religion, Government, and Religious Freedom" (Washington, D.C.: Americans United for Separation of Church and State), accessed October 23, 2011, http://www.au.org/resources/publica tions/is-america-a-christian-nation.

2. David L. Holmes, *The Faiths of the Founding Fathers* (New York: Oxford University Press, 2006), 46.

3. Clinton Rossiter, ed., *The Federalist Papers* (New York: New American Library, 1961), 322.

4. Edwin S. Gaustad, *Proclaim Liberty Throughout All the Land: A History of Church and State in America* (New York: Oxford University Press, 2003), 26.

5. *Walz v. Tax Commission of the City of New York*, 397 U.S. 664 (1970).

6. *Lemon v. Kurtzman,* 411 U.S. 192 (1973).

7. Roger Williams, as quoted in Daniel L. Dreisbach, *Thomas Jefferson and the Wall of Separation Between Church and State* (New York: New York University Press, 2002), 77.

8. For a more detailed discussion of a similar diagram and a quiz designed to help church leaders think more about their views on political engagement, see "The Church and Politics Quiz," *Leadership* 29, no. 3 (Summer 2008), 23–25.

Chapter 7: Connecting Faith and Politics: Different Christian Models

1. Robert Bellah, "Civil Religion in America," *Daedalus* 96, no. 11 (1967).

2. Dwight D. Eisenhower, "Statement by the President Upon Signing Bill To Include the Words 'Under God' in the Pledge to the Flag," June 14, 1954, in *The American Presidency Project*, eds. Gerhard Peters and John T. Woolley, accessed June 20, 2011, http://www.presidency.ucsb.edu/ws/?pid=9920.

3. Roderick P. Hart, *Campaign Talk: Why Elections Are Good for Us* (Princeton, NJ: Princeton University Press, 2000), 48–49.

4. See, for example, Roderick Hart, *The Political Pulpit* (West Lafayette, IN: Purdue University Press, 1977); Cynthia Toolin, "American Civil Religion from 1789–1981: A Content Analysis of Presidential Inaugural Addresses," *Review of Religious Research* 25 (1983): 39–48; and Michael Waldman, *POTUS Speaks: Finding the Words that Defined the Clinton Presidency* (New York: Simon & Schuster, 2000).

5. Clarke Cochran, "Life on the Border," in *Church, State, and Public Justice: Five Views*, ed. P. C. Kemeny (Downers Grove, IL: IVP Academic, 2007), 45.

6. *Catechism of the Catholic Church* (Allen, TX: Thomas More, 1994), 540–41.

7. *Forming Consciences for Faithful Citizens: A Call to Political Responsibility from the Catholic Bishops of the United States* (Washington, D.C.: U.S. Conference of Catholic Bishops, 2011), 13–17, accessed October 26, 2011, http://www.usccb.org/issues-and-action/faithful-citizenship/upload/forming-consciences-for-faithful-citizenship.pdf.

8. Kristin E. Heyer, "Insights from Catholic Social Ethics and Political Participation," in *Toward an Evangelical Public Policy*, eds. Ron Sider and Diane Knippers (Grand Rapids, MI: Baker, 2005), 105.

9. Cochran, 42.

10. Heyer, 104.

11. As quoted in David C. Steinmetz, *Luther in Context* (Bloomington, IN: Indiana University Press, 1986), 121.

12. Ibid., 115.

13. *Render unto Caesar . . . and unto God: A Lutheran View of Church and State* (St. Louis, MO: The Commission on Theology and Church Relations of the Lutheran Church–Missouri Synod, 1995), 67.

14. Werner O. Packull, "An Introduction to Anabaptist Theology," in *The Cambridge Companion to Reformation Theology*, eds. David Bagchi and David C. Steinmetz (Cambridge: Cambridge University Press, 2004), 214–15.

15. Ibid., 209.

16. Ronald J. Sider, "An Anabaptist Perspective on Church, Government, Violence, and Politics," *Brethren in Christ History and Life* 28, no. 2 (2005): 255.

17. Walter Klaassen, ed., *Anabaptism in Outline: Selected Primary Sources* (Scottdale, PA: Herald Press, 1981), 245.

18. Hans Denck, "Concerning True Love," 1527, excerpted in Klaassen, 250.

19. Corwin Smidt, "Principled Pluralist Perspective," in Kemeny, 131.

20. Ibid., 133.

21. David C. Steinmetz, *Calvin in Context* (New York: Oxford University Press, 1995), 204–5.

22. Ibid., 143–44.

Chapter 8: From Diatribe to Dialogue: How to Disagree about Politics Peacefully

1. For the complete text of the letter, see http://www.demossnews.com/resources/civility_project.pdf.

2. "Leonard Lance Avoids the Crucial Question," http://www.bluejersey.com/diary/9247/.

3. David Walker and Robert Bixby, "National Fiscal Dialogue Needed," *Politico*, May 6, 2011, accessed July 6, 2011, http://www.politico.com/news/stories/0511/54369.html.

Chapter 9: Can Christians Honestly Disagree? Applying Faith to Policy Problems

1. Katia McGlynn, "The Funniest Signs from the Rally to Restore Sanity/Fear," *Huffington Post*, November 1, 2010, accessed July 26, 2011, http://www.huffingtonpost.com/2010/10/30/the-funniest-signs-at-the_n_776490.html#s170117&title=Wheres_the_candy.

2. Liz Brown, "Rally to Restore Sanity—Jon Stewart's Closing Speech," *Examiner.com*, October 30, 2010, accessed July 26, 2011, http://www.examiner.com/celebrity-in-national/rally-to-restore-sanity-jon-stewart-s-closing-speech-full-text.

3. Daniel J. Treier, "Proof Text," in *Dictionary for Theological Interpretation of the Bible*, ed. Kevin Vanhoozer (Grand Rapids, MI: Baker Academic, 2005), 623.

4. One possible resource for further study is Craig Blomberg, *Neither Poverty nor Riches: A Biblical Theology of Possessions* (Downers Grove, IL: IVP Academic, 2001).

5. The primary formula for calculating poverty statistics is decades old and highly contested. More than likely, the numbers underestimate the income needed to meet basic needs. For the purpose of this short discussion, however, I will rely on these measures.

6. U.S. Census Bureau, *Income, Poverty and Health Insurance Coverage in the United States: 2010* (Washington, D.C.: U.S. Census Bureau, September 13, 2011), accessed September 23, 2011, http://www.census.gov/newsroom/releases/archives/income_wealth/cb11-157.html.

7. Calculated from Arloc Sherman, "Despite Deep Recession and High

Unemployment, Government Efforts—Including the Recovery Act—Prevented Poverty from Rising in 2009, New Census Data Show" (Washington, D.C.: Center for Budget and Policy Priorities, January 5, 2011), accessed July 28, 2011, http://www.cbpp.org/cms/index.cfm?fa=view &id=3361.

8. Matthew Ladner, "How to Win the War on Poverty: An Analysis of State Poverty Trends," *Policy Report*, no. 215 (Phoenix, AZ: Goldwater Institute, 2006), accessed October 22, 2011, http://goldwaterinstitute.org/sites/default/files/PovertyStudy_0.pdf.

9. Anisha Desai, Scott Klinger, Gloribell Mota, and Liz Stanton, *Nothing to Be Thankful For: Tax Cuts and the Deteriorating U.S. Job Market* (Boston: United for a Fair Economy, November 2005, revised January 2006), accessed July 29, 2011, http://faireconomy.org/files/pdf/No_Thanks_Report_01_06.pdf.

10. *A Circle of Protection: A Statement on Why We Need to Protect Programs for the Poor* (Washington, D.C.: Circle of Protection, April 27, 2011), accessed online July 28, 2011, http://www.circleofprotection.us/pdf/Circle-of-Protection-Statement.pdf.

11. Jonathan Weisman and Alan Cooperman, "A Religious Protest Largely from the Left," *Washington Post*, December 14, 2005, accessed July 28, 2011, http://www.washingtonpost.com/wp-dyn/content/article/2005/12/13/AR2005121301764.html.

12. U.S. Department of Housing and Urban Development, "Fiscal Year 2010 Continuum of Care Grants Awards" (Washington, D.C.: U.S. Department of Housing and Urban Development, January 10, 2011), accessed July 29, 2011, http://portal.hud.gov/hudportal/HUD?src=/program_offices/comm_planning/homeless/budget/2010.

13. Carol Towarnicky, "Why the Budget Is a Moral Document," *Philadelphia Daily News*, January 17, 2007, accessed October 22, 2001, http://articles.philly.com/2007-01-17/news/25220338_1_minimum-wage-moral-values-faith.

Chapter 10: Ready, Set, Vote! A Decision-Making Guide

1. Elizabeth Anne Oldmixon, *Uncompromising Positions: God, Sex, and the U.S. House of Representatives* (Washington, D.C.: Georgetown University Press, 2005).

2. Christian Coalition of America, *2010 Senate Votes* (Washington, D.C.: Christian Coalition of America), accessed July 12, 2011, http://cc.org/files/13/2010Scorecard8_5x11.pdf.

★ ★ ★

Acknowledgments

Every worthwhile writing project benefits from the assistance, encouragement, and support of many people. I am grateful to each person, named and unnamed, who has helped me with some aspect of preparing this manuscript. The book is better for their contributions. As is always the case, the mistakes that remain are mine alone.

I am grateful for mentors who have supported me in my career and helped shape my understanding of politics. My undergraduate adviser, John J. Pitney Jr., is a constant and faithful source of encouragement. My senior colleague at Wheaton College, Mark Amstutz, is a wonderful model of what it means to integrate faith and learning; he inspired me to devote more time to writing projects designed to serve the church.

Many people contributed to this project in important ways. I am grateful for the enthusiasm that Barnabas Piper, Betsey Newenhuyse, and Adam Kellogg exhibited from the very beginning of the process. They share my vision that followers of Christ can and should engage in meaningful but charitable political dialogue, and I am deeply grateful for their support. Brittany Biggs and many others on the team at Moody Publishers also helped make the process smooth and enjoyable. Rachel Vanderhill was a great help as I wrote the introduction to chapter 3, and Larycia Hawkins provided constructive feedback on several draft chapters. I owe additional thanks to Wheaton College students Jennifer Moretz and Eric Lowe for their capable research assistance and good humor, especially with mundane but essential formatting tasks.

Teresa Duncan, office coordinator extraordinaire, read every chapter, cheered me on, and offered practical help. I also want to acknowledge Provost Stanton Jones and the G. W. Aldeen Fund at Wheaton College for essential funding that helped me complete this project and meet my deadlines.

Last, and certainly not least, I would like to acknowledge my family and the ways they support me personally and as I seek to live out my vocational calling. My parents and sister read everything I write and love me anyway. My husband, Dan, is a source of great strength and support. He reads my drafts with a keen yet gentle editorial eye. When deadlines approach, he tolerates the significant increase in take-out dinners and devises extra excursions with Anna to give me more writing time. Most importantly, he is a wonderful model of what it means to honor God with humility, grace, and reason. My daughter, Anna, is a constant reminder of God's faithfulness. She keeps me laughing and brings joy to even the most mundane of tasks. It is to her that I warmly dedicate this book with my prayers that she will honor God all of her days.

AMY E. BLACK
Wheaton, Illinois

AN ERA HAS ENDED

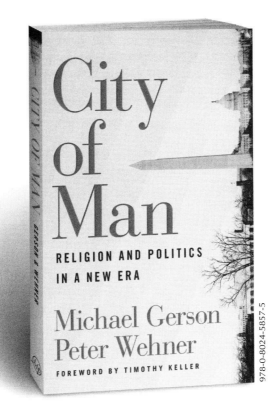

The political movement that most galvanized evangelicals for more than a quarter-century, the Religious Right, is fading away. What lies ahead is unclear.

Into this uncertainty, former White House insiders Michael Gerson and Peter Wehner call evangelicals toward a new kind of political engagement—a kind that is better both for the church and the country, a kind that cannot be co-opted by either political party, a kind that avoids the historic mistakes of both the Religious Right and the Religious Left.